THE SONG OF ROLAND

THE SONG OF ROLAND
translated with an introduction by
C. H. Sisson

 CARCANET PRESS / MANCHESTER

First published in 1983 by
CARCANET PRESS LIMITED
210 Corn Exchange Buildings
Manchester M4 3BQ

British Library Cataloguing in Publication Data

[La Chanson de Roland. *English*] .   The song of Roland
  I. The song of Roland   II. Sisson, C.H.
  841'.1   PQ1521.E5

ISBN 0-85635-421-X

The publisher acknowledges the financial assistance of
the Arts Council of Great Britain

Printed in England by SRP Ltd., Exeter

CONTENTS

INTRODUCTION

THE story of the *Chanson de Roland* has its origin in the obscure history of the eighth century. In 778 Charlemagne, then the most powerful figure in the western world, undertook an expedition into Spain, which was already largely over-run by Muslims from North Africa. Although in the *Chanson* this enterprise is represented as a crusade, this was hardly the nature of it. The year before, Charlemagne had been approached by some of these intruders, who had sought his help against their co-religionists further south in the country, and it was in response to this appeal that he ventured over the Pyrenees. Moreover—and contrary to what the *Chanson* tells us—the expedition was not a success. Charlemagne took Pamplona, a Christian city, and afterwards razed it to the ground. Before Saragossa, which was held by the Saracens, he failed, and had to turn back to meet trouble nearer home. It was during this withdrawal that, in the narrow pass of the Roncesvalles, the rear-guard was ambushed and Roland, the Warden of the Breton Marches, was killed—not by Saracens, as the story is told, but by Basques who no doubt saw an opportunity for plunder. Out of this slender material the epic of *Roland* was made, but not before the passage of time had made it possible to improve on history without fear of contradiction.

It seems that the chroniclers, both Christian and Muslim, are laconic on the subject, neither party finding in the events much that they wished to advertise. The antecedents of the poem itself have been the subject of much enquiry and much argument by scholars since the work first re-emerged into the light of day in the first half of the nineteenth century, but the findings, truth to tell, are largely negative. The authorship has been the subject of debate. All in all, there seems to be no sufficient reason for the ordinary reader not to take it that the poem is the work of one Turoldus, who in effect signs it in the last lines. He was a poet of great genius and originality. The *Chanson de Roland* is not only the first, but incomparably the best, of the *chansons de geste*. It stands as it were on the threshold of French literature, the first great work we encounter. We have the *Cantilène d'Eulalie* of the ninth century:

Buona pulcella fut Eulalia,
Bel auret corps, bellezour anima.

In the tenth and eleventh centuries we have—less impressively
—the lives of St Leger and St Alexis. The date of the *Chanson
de Roland*—another subject of controversy—is certainly some-
where in the neighbourhood of 1100.

What we have, therefore, in the *Chanson*, is a re-handling,
about the time of the First Crusade, of events from the age of
Charlemagne. This meant that the author of the poem was
much more preoccupied with the notion of a Christendom
set against the pagan world than could have been the case in
the eighth century. If the events are those of the earlier time,
the sentiments, one might say the politics, are those of the
later. The matter is more complicated than that, however.
Whatever the precise pre-history of the story of the *Chanson*,
there is no doubt that during the three or more centuries that
had passed since Charlemagne's expedition the heroes of it
had become larger than life. It is not a falsification of history
that Turoldus gives us but a world of legend, yet it is a legend
around which enough reality still clings to engage not only a
sense of wonder but a sense of actuality. That this double
effect still operates on us at the present time is due to the
poet's profound grasp of his themes. He understands these
characters who think nothing is more creditable than to split
someone's brains in two or to raze a city to the ground, and
exhibits great sophistication in his delineation of their loyal-
ties and jealousies. One is reminded again and again of that
singular combination of vigour and clarity of line which
marks Romanesque architecture and sculpture. Anyone who
has mooched around churches in England or France knows
how the work of the period stands out among the still beauti-
ful but fussier work of the later Middle Ages. All this grace,
strength and sureness of touch are to be found in the work of
Turoldus.

The story moves with great rapidity, for Turoldus does
not give us more than the essentials. A sight of the high
mountains and the deep valleys of the passes, of Ganelon
throwing back his marten-skins in a moment of anger, are
given us in a flash. Charlemagne's councils, the councils of

the pagan king Marsilie, are presented so that we see the actors and feel the ominous weight of the business transacted. The battle scenes are told as by someone who 'remembers with advantages' what feats were done there, but the exaggerations are never allowed to destroy the solidity of the actors. When Roland and Oliver die after the desperate battle in the Roncevalles, it is not as over-sized heroes, but as any pair of young comrades-in-arms dying in a far country after having done their uttermost. The *Chanson* is a sombre and relentless poem, as well as an extraordinarily lively one. Fantastic in some respects, it is in a profound sense true not only to the spirit of the times from which it emerged, with their absolute and menacing demands and feudal loyalties, but to that of any time in which violence is not far away.

There are invincible oddities. The Saracens are represented as idolaters, who smash up their gods when they fail them. Charlemagne is not merely the emperor, but a sort of priest-king who can give absolution to his men at the start of a great enterprise. There is a world of darkness and ignorance under the glittering surface of the poem, but it is because rather than in spite of this that we are left with so strong an impression of the depth and grasp of the poet's mind.

The strangeness and remoteness of the world from which the legend, and the poem itself, well up, present some difficulties to the translator. For in a translation the *tone* is, if not everything, at least something he must be sure of, if he is to produce a version which carries any conviction. This is a matter not of conscious working out—whatever work the translator may have to put in on details of the text—but of direct perception. The translator has to feel at home with the mind of the author; he has also—and this is the translator's difficulty *par excellence*—to see how he can say the things the author says in the language of an utterly different time, moving among utterly different superficial assumptions, whatever profound affinities may lurk below. The world of Lucretius and Catullus, or of Horace and Virgil, was very different from our own, but these poets were at the centre of a great urban civilization, full of sophistication of the kind we understand. The world of Dante was different again, but however strange his cosmology may be to us, the people he presents to us so vividly have all the concerns which still lie at the heart of our civilization. With the world of Roland things are otherwise. Turoldus's sharp delineation of character is such that, despite the unfamiliar circumstances we can recognize the types we know, but their assumptions and the general content of their minds are so unlike our own that it is hard to pick the language in which we could talk to them. What does one say to a man whose greatest glory is to hit someone else over the head, or to be the leading hand in a massacre, and who thinks it natural that a traitor should be pulled limb from limb by cavorting stallions? These things are not as far from us as we should like to think, but they are pleasures from which we avert at least our conversation. The solution of using a garbled and sham antique language, which no one ever spoke, to suggest that people were different in those old times, is not open to us—at least if we believe in the continuing life of old literatures and the radical unchangeability of the human race. One has to learn to live with the assumptions of heroic legend without finding them all that strange; and in fact, they are not that strange.

The qualities of the language and verse of the poem present us with difficulties of a lesser but by no means negligible order. The Old French or Norman-French in which it is written had emerged over the preceding centuries from the vulgar Latin spoken by Caesar's soldiers and the colonists, with some admixtures. What Turoldus gives us is a speech of comparatively limited vocabulary, by modern standards, as it were presided over by radical Latin meanings which had changed colour more or less with the passage of time and the development of the feudal and ecclesiastical systems. So narrow a range is not easily accommodated in the English of our own day, but at least it points in the direction of a language as simple and direct as may be. As to the verse, there can be no question of adopting exactly the form of the original, though something like that has been attempted in more than one twentieth-century version. The *Chanson* is written in what are called *laisses*—bundles or stanzas—of ten-syllabled assonanced verse. This may call for as many as twenty or thirty rhymes or half-rhymes in a stanza—an absurdity in modern English and one which is bound to distort the language so that anything like a natural directness is lost. As to the number of syllables, the classic line in French is of twelve syllables, and it is this which corresponds to the classic English line of ten syllables. The ten-syllable line in French is a *short* line, and the nearest equivalent in English is the line of eight syllables. A great deal more of the speed of the original—an essential characteristic one may reasonably hope to preserve in translation—is lost by ignoring this point. Given all these considerations, my solution has been to use a basic octosyllabic couplet, not however counting on my fingers for every line.

I first became interested in the *Chanson de Roland* through Joseph Bédier's edition of the Oxford manuscript and this edition, with its sensitive prose version *en face*, is probably still the best starting point for anyone who has access to modern French and wishes to explore the text further. The essential supplement is the volume of commentaries Bédier published some years later (in 1927). Bédier is at once immensely scholarly and immensely literate, and his work has an enduring attraction for the general student of literature. Of course debate did not cease with his volumes. Among more recent books I have consulted are Paul Aebischer's *Préhistoire et protohistoire du Roland d'Oxford* (Berne, 1972) and André Burger's *Turold, poète de la fidelité* (Geneva, 1977).

My version was commissioned by the BBC in 1981 and originally broadcast on Radio 3 in October and November 1982 with brilliant incidental music by Nigel Osborne. I should like to thank Fraser Steel, to whose grasp of its literary, dramatic and musical possibilities the project owed so much from its inception, as well as the actors, Garard Green, Christopher Neame, Andy Rashleigh, Geoffrey Banks, Ann Rye, Bert Parnaby and above all John Franklyn-Robbins, the narrator, for the manner in which they made it come to life.

C. H. SISSON

1   THE king, our emperor Charlemagne
Has been for seven years in Spain
And conquered it right to the sea.
Not a castle, wall or city
Is left standing, except one
And that is Saragossa town,
Up a mountain. The misbelieving
Marsilie holds it, the pagan king.
A bad end comes to those who follow,
Like him, Mahomet and Apollo.

2   In Saragossa, king Marsilie
Is in a shady orchard. He
Lies upon blue marble and
Has twenty thousand men at hand.
He calls his dukes and counts and says:
'My lords, are we not in distress?
The emperor from that sweet France
Has led our country such a dance.
My army can't stand up to his,
No matter how courageous ours is.
You are supposed to give advice:
Can you say which way safety lies?'
No single pagan responds
Except Blancandrins from Val-Fonde.

3   Blancandrins is the wisest man
The pagans have, and no one can
Outdo him in counsel or in fight.
He says: 'No occasion for fright!
Charles is vain, you have only to send
Your submission and say you are his friend.
Give him bears and dogs and lions,
Seven hundred camels, a thousand falcons,
Four hundred mules with silver and gold

13

And fifty waggons with all they'll hold:
Then tell him it's time he went away.
Enough fighting, tell him; he'd as well
Go back now to Aix-la-Chapelle.
You will follow him, say, at Michaelmas
And become a Christian without fuss
And admit that all the honour is his:
If he wants, he can have hostages
—Ten or twenty thousand should reassure him
We would send our sons, if that would fool him.
They may be killed, but I'll send mine.
Better that they should have a rough time
Than that we should be dishonoured and beg
At the end of our days for a bit of bread.'

4   Blancandrins says: 'By my right hand
And by my beard, you would see the land
Rid of the French in no time at all.
The Franks would go back to France, the small
Men to their villages, Charles himself
Would soon be home in Aix-la-Chapelle.
At Michaelmas, there'd be a great do,
The day would arrive—and end too—
Without there being a sign of us.
The king of course would be furious;
He would have off the hostages' heads.
Better that they should be dead
Than that we should lose the whole of Spain
And never be our own masters again.'
'He may be right,' the pagans say.

5   Marsilie's council is at an end.
He calls ten of his special friends
And biggest rascals: first, Clarin,
Estamarin and Eudropin,
Priam, and Guarlan with the beard,
Then five more who are not less feared

—Machiner, and his uncle Maheu,
Jouner, Malbien, no one knew
And Blancandrins. He gives them orders:
'You, barons, will go to Cordres;
Charles is now besieging it.
Take olive branches. Have the wit
To look like men who come in peace.
A touch of deference would please.
Reach an agreement and I'll give
You gold and silver as long as I live
And fiefs, if you like, and land.'
The pagans say: 'We understand.'

6   King Marsilie's council is done;
He tells his barons to be gone.
'Carry branches of olive, make
Charles think that for his God's sake
He ought to have mercy on me.
Tell him that next month he'll see
A thousand of us with him, come
To take the law of Christendom
And I will swear to be his man.
If he wants to have hostages, he can.'
'That should work,' says Blancandrins.

7   Marsilie sends for ten white mules,
A present from the king of Santule.
They have silver saddles on their backs;
The messengers mount and hit the track.
Each of them carries an olive branch.
They are going to Charles, who rules France.
He must believe them. He hasn't a chance.

8   The emperor is happy now.
The walls of Cordres are all down;
His catapaults have smashed the towers;
His knights have helped themselves to spoil,

Gold, silver and expensive arms.
Not a pagan left the city,
All dead or gone over to Christianity.
The emperor is in an orchard,
Roland and Oliver with him, assorted
Barons, Samson the duke, Anseïs
Who is so full of his own fleas,
Geoffrey of Anjou who carries the king's
Flag and—together in everything—
Gerin and Gerer, with many more.
There are fifteen thousand of them all told;
Sweet France has no better knights.
All around they sit on white
Silken carpets. They all amuse
Themselves as they like; the old men choose
Chess, while the young men play with swords.
Under a pine and beside a thorn
A throne of gold has been erected.
There sits the king with his respected
Snowy beard and trailing hair
Who rules all France and has the air,
With his strong frame and haughty looks
Of being who he is. The crooks
Who come from Marsilie dismount
And give a plausible account
Of who they are. They begin the meeting
With well-designed and loving greetings.

9   Blancandrins is the first to speak:
'God save the king!' he says, 'I mean
The God whom all of us should adore.
Marsilie wanted to know more
About the law which brings salvation;
And now sends presents from our nation:
Bears and lions, greyhounds on the leash,
Seven hundred camels, the best in all the east,
A thousand falcons, and four hundred mules

Loaded with gold and silver, waggons too,
A train of fifty of them. Enough to pay
Your soldiers and see them happy on their way.
For you have been here long enough. To go
To France and Aix must have attractions now.
My king is anxious now to follow you.'
The emperor stretches up his hands to God
And bows his head. He is lost in thought.

10   The emperor keeps his head down.
He is not quick to use his mouth.
His custom is to speak at leisure;
He looks up to make known his pleasure.
He says to the messengers: 'Well said:
But king Marsilie is not my friend,
How can I trust a word he says?'
The Saracens answer: 'Hostages!
Ten, fifteen, twenty if you will;
I will risk my son being killed
And there'll be better born than he.
Then when you're back in your palace you'll see
At Michaelmas—Michael de periculo—
The emperor will have followed you.
In the baths God made you at Aix
He will be baptised for Christ's sake.'
Charles replies: 'He could still be saved.'

11   It's a fine evening, with a clear sky.
Charles has the ten mules led away.
Then, for the messengers, a tent
Is set in an orchard. Ten sergeants
Fix them up with all they need.
The emperor is up at first light;
Hears mass and mattins, then goes straight
To council under a pine tree.
He calls the barons of France, for he
Wants to know what they approve
And without that he will not move.

12 There the king sits under his pine-tree
  And calls all his nobility:
  Ogier, duke, Turpin, archbishop,
  Young Henry and ancient Richard,
  The count of Gascony, Acelin,
  Tibbald of Rheims with Milon his cousin
  And Gerer and Gerin. Then here they are,
  The famous Roland and Oliver,
  One is brave and the other wise:
  And more than a thousand Franks besides:
  Ganelon, who betrayed his friends.
  This counsel came to a bad end.

13 'My lords,' the king begins, 'You see:
  I've heard from that king Marsilie.
  He wants to give me a great mass
  Of his belongings, such creatures as
  Bears and lions and hunting dogs,
  Seven hundred camels and a thousand hawks,
  Four hundred mules, with all the Arab
  Gold the animals can carry,
  And more loaded in fifty carts.
  So far so good. The other part
  Of his message is, that I should go
  Back to France, to Aix and so
  Give him the chance to follow me
  And embrace Christianity
  —To be baptised and hold the marches.
  How can I know where his heart is?'
  The French say: 'We can be on our guard.'

14 The emperor has had his say.
  Roland's thoughts turn the other way.
  He jumps to his feet to contradict:
  'You will regret it quickly
  If you believe Marsilie again.
  Seven years we have been in Spain:

Why have I conquered all these cities
For you, Noplès and Commiblès?
Taken Valerne and the land of Pine,
Balaguer, Tuele and Sezille?
Marsilie was a traitor then:
He sent you fifteen pagan men,
Each of them with an olive twig
And a pack of lies that were just as big
As those he is offering to you now,
And you let your Frenchmen tell you how
You should behave, and they talked like fools.
Although you knew the pagans were cruel
You sent them two counts, Basilie
And Basan and, by Haltilie
They had their heads off. How can you not
Carry the war on, after that?
Lay siege to Saragossa if
It takes you all the rest of your life.
Basan and Basilie were our friends:
And now, by God, they should be avenged.'

15   The emperor doesn't look up.
He strokes his beard and then he tugs
His moustache, and says nothing
To all his nephew's blustering.
The French keep quiet, all except
Ganelon—and up he gets
There, in front of the emperor:
'What is all this clatter for?
Why should you believe anyone,
Me or another, unless there is some
Advantage in it for the king?
If Marsilie means anything
When he says he will be your man
And do homage to you for Spain,
Becoming a Christian into the bargain,
Is that something we ought to argue?

Anyone who, because of pride,
Wants to set such an offer aside
Cannot care how we die. Such impudence,
To set aside all common prudence!'

16   After that Naimès comes, the court
Has no better vassal than this lord.
He says to the king: 'Now you have heard
What Ganelon said; they were sensible words.
The matter should be debated no more.
King Marsilie has lost the war;
You have taken his castles, your catapaults
Have left enormous holes in his walls;
His cities have been set alight,
His men are left without much fight.
When he sends and asks for mercy,
With hostages as guarantee,
You ought to grant it; there is no more
Reason to continue this war.'
The French say: 'So it is;
He has spoken well, Duke Naimès.'

17   'My lords, barons, who shall go
To see what king Marsilie's up to?'
Duke Naimès says: 'You can send me.
Your glove and stick are all I need.'
The king replies: 'You were not asked.
By my beard and my moustache
You shall not go so far away;
I might need your advice one day.
Go and sit down.' The duke obeys.

18   'My lords, barons, whom shall we send
To see that wily Saracen
Who still holds Saragossa town?'
Then Roland answers: 'I'll go down!'
'You won't!' exclaims count Oliver,

'With your arrogance and quick temper
You'll pick a quarrel before you start.
I should be better in that part.
If the king wishes, I will go.'
Charles says: 'Shut up, the pair of you!
Neither goes. Let it be clear
I will send none of the twelve peers.
God help anyone who proposes
That.' The French looked down their noses.

19   Turpin interrupts from the ranks.
'Why do you reproach your Franks?'
He said to the king. 'They have been here,
With pain and effort, for seven years.
Give me the stick and glove, I'll go
And I'll soon see what sort of man
He is, this Spanish Saracen.'
The emperor shouts: 'Go and sit down
On your white silk and hold your tongue.
I don't want to hear another sound!'

20   'You Frankish knights,' says the emperor
And rather pointedly ignores
The archbishop: 'Propose somebody
Who comes from my own territory
And who can go to Marsilie.'
Roland says: 'Ganelon, my step-father!'
The French say: 'There is none we would rather
Propose. He is the wisest man.'
But did that upset Ganelon?
He threw his marten-skins back from
His throat in fury. He has on
A tunic of white silk. His eyes
Are grey, his looks are full of pride;
He is well-built and elegant:
The French have found the man they want.
He says to Roland: 'Are you mad,

With all this talk of your step-father?
You hope you will get rid of me
By sending me to Marsilie;
If I come back there will be sparks:
You'll get a battering, and the marks
Will still be with you in old age.'
Roland replies: 'Oh, you can rage;
They all know threats are nothing to me.
Brains are needed for an embassy;
The king would prefer me, probably.'

21   Ganelon answers: 'You have the face
To say you will go in my place?
You are not my man nor I your lord.
Charles is the one who gives the orders!
Saragossa? Marsilie?
I will go, but you watch me:
I'll find a way of paying you off.'
At that, Roland began to laugh.

22   When Ganelon sees Roland laughing
It is as if he faced disaster;
He feels a burning anger, which
Almost drives him out of his wits.
He says to the count: 'This is your doing;
I have the mission, you hope to ruin
Me by it. I hate you. But you are just,
Emperor; I will go, since I must.'

23   'Saragossa, then! I know that men
Who go there don't come back again.
My wife's your sister, don't forget,
I have a son, a fine well-set
Young lad, Baldwin. To him I leave
All my honours and my fiefs.
Look after him, for it is certain
I shan't set eyes on him again.'

Charles replies: 'Your heart's too tender.
Go and fix up the surrender.'

24   The king says: 'Ganelon, be quick,
Here, take from me my glove and stick.
You heard, the French have chosen you.'
Ganelon says: 'It was Roland's doing!
I'll have no love for him after this,
Nor for Oliver, that friend of his,
Nor for the twelve peers, they're too fond of him.
Before you I defy the lot of them!'
The king says: 'You speak bitterly.
But you'll go, you have orders from me.'
'I'll go, but it's without guarantee,
Like Basan and his brother Basilie.'

25   The emperor held out his glove
But Ganelon was slow to move
And when he should have taken it,
It fell. The French say: 'What is this?
What does it mean? Loss, probably.'
Ganelon says: 'You will hear from me.'

26   'Sir,' says Ganelon, 'Give me your blessing.
Since I must go, no point in messing.'
The king says: 'Now, in Jesus' name
And in my name, go!' And at the same
Time he makes the sign of the cross,
Absolves him, and sends him off,
Handing him, before he goes,
The stick and a diplomatic note.

27   Ganelon goes back to his tent
And puts together his equipment,
Taking the best of everything:
Golden spurs, and soon he is buckling
His sword Margleis. He mounts upon

His favourite charger, Tachebrun.
Guenemer holds the stirrup;
There is weeping among the troop
Of knights. They all say: 'Ah, my lord,
You have been so long at the king's court!
You are known to be a noble vassal.
The man who condemned you to this shall
Not get off scot-free, although
The king himself would have it so.
Count Roland should not have picked on you,
You're from too good a family!'
Then they say: 'Would you like company?
We'll come.' Ganelon replies:
'Oh, God, no. If one of us dies,
That is enough. You'll go back to France.
Speak to my wife if you have a chance
And to my old friend Pinabel
And of course to my son Baldwin as well
—He is your leader, from today.'
And with these words he rode away.

28   Under the olives rides Ganelon,
Following the messengers of the Saracens;
Blancandrins drops behind to be
With Ganelon and very wily
Their conversation is. Blancandrins
Says: 'He is a remarkable man,
Your Charles: Calabria conquered, Pouille!
England, the other side of the sea
Forced to pay up Peter's pence.
If I may say so without offence,
I wonder why he bothers with us.'
Ganelon answers: 'That's how it is.
Nobody like him. He's marvellous.'

29   Blancandrins says: 'I like the Franks
But their counts and dukes deserve no thanks

From Charles for the advice they give!
What a life they make him live!'
Ganelon answers: 'They're all right,
Except for Roland, who acts in spite.
One morning, when the king and a few
Of us were there in the shade, his nephew
Came along with his armour on
—Just back with spoil from Carcassonne.
He had a red apple in his hand:
"Here you are, uncle," said Roland and
"If you take a fancy to anyone's crown
Just tell me, I will bring it round."
His pride is like that, and every day
He puts his life at risk. I say
There'll be peace when he is put out of the way.'

30 Blancandrins says: 'Yes, Roland, he
Wants to make everyone cry for mercy,
No one else has rights of any sort.
Who does he count on for support?'
Ganelon answers: 'It's the French,
They love him. They've got no sense.
Of course, he gives them silver and gold,
Horses, everything. I'm told
Even the emperor takes what he can.
He wants to conquer the east, that man.'

31 As they ride on, Ganelon
And Blancandrins, they agree on
A compact: Roland must be killed.
They ride on tracks and paths until
They come to Saragossa town.
Under a yew-tree they dismount.
Under the shadow of a pine
Is a throne, enveloped in fine
Silk of Alexandrian grain:
On it is the king of Spain.

All around him, Saracens,
Twenty thousand silent men.
This is the news they want to hear
Now Ganelon and Blancandrins appear.

32   He goes to Marsilie, Blancandrins,
Holding Ganelon by the hand,
And says to the king: 'Mahomet bless
You, and holy Apollo not less!
And may we ever keep their laws!
We have done your embassy to Charles.
He raised his hands to heaven and swore
By his God, and said nothing more.
He has sent you a noble baron,
A Frenchman, an important man:
He will say whether you will have peace.'
Marsilie answers: 'Let him speak.'

33   Count Ganelon had thought about
How he should address the proud
King Marsilie, so he said:
'Blessings on your royal head
From the great God whom we adore;
Listen to this, from the emperor:
Receive the Christian law and he
Will give you half of Spain. But be
Stubborn and take the other course
And he will have you seized by force!
You will be taken back to Aix
And receive judgement in that place:
That means death, and a nasty one.'
King Marsilie begins to run
His fingers over the dart he holds
—An ugly weapon feathered with gold—
He would have thrown it, but his men
Encourage him to think again.

34   Marsilie changed colour and took
A tighter grip of the dart. He shook.
When Ganelon saw it, he put his hand
Upon the hilt of his sword and
Drew it two inches out of its scabbard.
'My lovely, my bright one, my best,' he murmured,
'I have carried you at the king's court.
No one in France shall ever report
I died alone in a strange country
Without the best of them crying for mercy!'
The pagans say: 'It will do no good
If this ends in shedding blood.'

35   And so the noblest Saracens
Get their king on his throne again.
The caliph says: 'It is not fit
That you should threaten the Frenchman. Better
To sit and hear what he has to say.
'Sir,' says Ganelon, 'If I may!
But don't suppose that all the gold
In Spain will stop me till I've told
The complete message that I bring
From Charles, the most powerful of kings,
To you, his mortal enemy.'
He is covered in furs and finery,
Sables and silk, he throws them down
(Blancandrins picks them from the ground)
But he keeps a firm hand on his sword
Which impresses the pagans even more.

36   Ganelon goes close to the king.
He says: 'It's no use blustering.
Charles, who is the master of France
Is certainly giving you a chance.
He says: Become a Christian
And he will give you half of Spain;
The other half goes to his nephew

27

Roland: a fine neighbour for you!
If you turn this offer down
He will at once besiege the town
Of Saragossa. The war will stop
When you are taken and tied up;
Then you'll be bundled off to Aix,
Not on a horse, I am to say,
Nor on a mule. He says you would
Go on a donkey like a load of wood.
There you would lose your head. You'd better
Have a look at the emperor's letter.'
And with that he hands it over
Like a billet-doux from a lover.

37   Marsilie is angry and turns pale.
He breaks and throws away the seal,
Looks at the note and sees what it says:
'Charles, king of France—and so on—refreshes
My memory about an incident
Which caused him great embarrassment,
When Basan and his brother Basilie
Lost their heads on the hill by Haltilie;
And adds, that if I value my life
I'd better send him my uncle, the caliph;
Otherwise he regrets—and so on.'
That was the cue for Marsilie's son.
He said to the king: 'He has gone too far.
But now that we have Ganelon here,
Let me have him to cut to pieces.'
When Ganelon hears this he releases
His sword from its scabbard and takes his stand
With his back to a pine-tree, as he had planned.

38   Marsilie goes to an orchard-place
With the best advisers that he has:
Blancandrins, with his snowy hair
And Jurfaret, his son and heir,

And the caliph, his uncle and minister.
Blancandrins says: 'Call Ganelon here;
He is our man; he has sworn to be.'
The king says: 'Bring him in, we'll see.'
Blancandrins brings him in. They find
What treason is in Ganelon's mind.

39   'Good sir Ganelon,' said Marsilie,
'I admit I treated you too lightly
When, in my anger, I threatened you.
Accept these marten skins, which truly
Are worth five hundred pounds in gold.
By tomorrow night you shall have your reward.'
Ganelon answers: 'I will not refuse.
And may God make it up to you!'

40   Marsilie said: 'Ah, I can tell
You and I will get on well,
Tell me about Charlemagne.
He is old, his time has gone
—Not less than two hundred years, I know.
He has exerted himself so,
In so many lands! So many blows
He has sustained upon his skull!
Fought in so many famous fields
And brought great kings to beggary!
When will he at last be weary?'
Ganelon answers: 'Charles is not
The man you think and anyone that
Sees and knows him understands
There is none like him in the land.
No words of mine can possibly give
Any idea how that man lives
Or what are his great qualities.
As for courage, I'd say that he's
The toughest man God ever made.
And he never refused a baron his aid.'

41   The pagan says: 'An astounding man,
Certainly, your Charlemagne.
But his age! No wonder I've been told
He's more than a couple of centuries old.
He's dragged his body around so far,
Through so many countries, got so many scars
And turned so many kings into beggars!
When will he give up? Or will he ever?'
'Not,' Ganelon says, 'while his nephew lives.
He's the best vassal a king could have.
His companion Oliver is a marvel;
And the twelve peers Charles loves so well
Form the vanguard, with twenty thousand knights.
Charles is safe and fears no man alive.'

42   The Saracen says: 'Astounding, yes,
Charlemagne. And his age not less
Than, as they say, two hundred years!
Wins wherever he goes, one hears;
Taken a few knocks, you say,
But all those kings left by the way!
When will he get tired of war?'
'Not while Roland lives, for sure,'
Says Ganelon. 'Go east, go west,
That man is always said to be best.
And then there's Oliver, his friend
And Charles's beloved twelve peers. They defend
Charles—with a few thousand knights.
Oh yes, Charles is safe, all right.'

43   'Good sir,' said Marsilie
To Ganelon, 'you should see my army;
I've got four hundred thousand knights.
Now with them I can surely fight
Charles and the French?' But Ganelon
Replies: 'You couldn't take them on,
You'd lose a lot of pagans that way.

Better be cautious. It would pay
To send the emperor such presents
The French gasp at their magnificence;
And send him twenty hostages,
He'll be off to France as soon as you please.
He'll have to leave a rear-guard behind;
His nephew will be in it, you'll find,
And Oliver. If you listen to me
Those two counts will be dead men.
Charles's great pride will be no more
And he will lose his taste for war.'

44   'Sir Ganelon,' asks Marsilie,
'How can I be sure Roland will die?'
'Listen to me,' Ganelon answers.
'The king will be in the frontier passes,
Roland will be away in the rear
And with him his friend Oliver.
There will be twenty thousand French.
Put in a hundred thousand men:
In a first battle you can hope
To leave the French in pretty poor shape:
I don't say your losses will be light,
But the second battle should be all right.
You'll get Roland in one or the other
And after that there'll be no more bother.
You'll get credit for winning the war
And as long as you live there'll be no more.

45   'If anyone could kill Roland, that man
Would deprive Charles of his right hand;
No more great armies after that;
Charles's recruiting would fall flat
And the old country would have a rest.'
Marsilie falls on Ganelon's neck
And kisses him, then lets him see
The contents of his treasury.

46   Marsilie said: 'We may agree
But that is hardly a guarantee.
I want you to swear that you will betray
Roland.' And what does Ganelon say?
'As you like.' Then on the relics
In his sword-hilt he swears a quick
Oath and is already foresworn.
It was a bad day when he was born.

47   There was a throne of ivory
And on it sat king Marsilie.
He had them bring a book, Mahomet's
And there before him it was set.
He swore, that Spanish Saracen
That if he or any of his men
Find Roland in the rear-guard, they
Will take him on and, if they may,
Kill him. Ganelon, eager too,
Says softly: 'May your wish come true.'

48   Then comes the pagan Valdabron
And stands before Marsilie's throne.
Relaxed, he laughs and offers his sword
To Ganelon, with friendly words:
'Here, take it, you won't find better than that,
The hilt alone is worth a lot.
With your help it should go hard
With Roland if he is in the rear-guard.'
'He'll be there all right,' says Ganelon.
They kiss one another on cheeks and chin.

49   Then the pagan Climorin, laughing too,
Says to Ganelon: 'Maybe you
Would like my helmet. It is the best
I ever saw. I should like to express
My gratitude for your advice;
We shan't need such a tip-off twice.'

Ganelon answers: 'It will work out.'
They kiss one another on cheeks and mouth.

50   Then it's the turn of Bramimond,
The queen. She says to Ganelon:
'Someone my husband and his men
Think so well of, must be my friend.
I'd like to send your wife two necklaces,
One amethysts, the other jacinths,
Both set in gold, and even in Rome
There are none more expensive, nor at home
In France, in your emperor's box of jewels.'
He pockets them; he is no fool.

51   The king calls Malduit the treasurer:
'Is the stuff for Charles all put together?'
He answers: 'Yes, sir. I've just been told:
Seven hundred camels, with silver and gold,
With the twenty hostages, and these
All come from distinguished families.'

52   Marsilie takes Ganelon by the shoulder
And says to him: 'You're a very fine soldier,
And prudent. So, by your gods and mine,
Don't change your tactics a second time.
I'm giving you a mass of gold,
Ten mules loaded with it. I've told
My men to send you the same every year.
I've got the keys of the city here:
Put king Charles in full possession
And make quite sure of Roland's position
In the rear-guard. When he's well behind
In a pass or defile, I've only to find
Him there and he will have his battle.'
Ganelon answers: 'I won't dawdle.'
There is nothing more for him to say;
He gets on his horse and rides away.

53   The emperor is back in his quarters.
He has come to the city of Galne with his soldiers:
Count Roland has taken it and destroyed it;
For a hundred years men will avoid it.
The king is waiting for Ganelon
And all the tribute he brings from Spain.
At dawn, there is a horse's tramp:
Count Ganelon arrives in camp.

54   The emperor is up early. He hears
Mass and matins. Then he appears
On the green grass before his tent.
Roland is there and with him his friend
Oliver. There is Naimès the duke
And many others and then, look!
Here comes Ganelon, the perjurer.
The wily man talks like a traitor:
He says to the king: 'God save your majesty!
I have brought back the keys to the city
Of Saragossa, as these
Treasures, and twenty hostages
Who should go under guard. It is not the king's fault
His uncle the caliph has not been caught.
I saw the caliph making off;
He had four hundred thousand tough
Troops around him, all ready armed
To see that he didn't come to harm
And to keep away from Christianity
Which they saw the risk of, with Marsilie.
But when they'd sailed four leagues or so
They were caught in a storm, and there is no
Possible doubt they were all drowned.
Had the caliph survived, he would have been found.
As for the pagan king, he wants
To follow you to your headquarters in France
And there, he will become a Christian
And formally swear to be your man

And to rule Spain as your dependent.'
The king says: 'Thank God for so ending
The war; you have done very well;
I shan't forget this.' Then he tells
A thousand trumpeters to sound
Their trumpets so that all around
His army pack their bags, strike camp
And start off on the road to France.

55   Charlemagne has beaten Spain down,
Taken castles and sacked the towns.
'That's that war finished,' thinks the king
As he rides towards France that evening.
. . . . .
Meanwhile Count Roland sticks his flag
On top of a hill; his troops encamp
In all the country round about.
Somewhere upon open ground
The pagans are riding, helmets laced,
Swords in belts, and shields in place
About their necks. Each has a lance.
They halt on a wooded eminence,
Four hundred thousand waiting for dawn.
God! if only the French were warned!

56   The day has vanished. It is deep
Night and the emperor is asleep.
He dreams that he is in a pass
Carrying his ash-wood lance.
Ganelon suddenly snatches it,
Brandishes and breaks it to bits;
The splinters scatter in the sky.
Charlemagne sleeps on peacefully.

57   Another dream. This time he is
In his chapel in Aix, and there he sees
A bear who bites at his right arm.

From the Ardennes direction, hard
On this there comes a leopard who
Goes fiercely for his heart. Then through
The hall there races a hound,
Coming to Charles by leaps and bounds.
He bites the bear's right ear off, then
Attacks the leopard. All the Frenchmen
Standing round say: 'A great battle!'
Who will win it is not settled.
So it goes on and all the time
Charles sleeps on and gives no sign.

58   The night has gone. In the clear dawn,
Amidst his army, the emperor rides on.
'My lords,' he says, 'Look at the passes
And narrow defiles!' The question he asks is:
'Whom shall we put in the rear-guard?' One
Answer comes quickly—from Ganelon:
'Roland, my step-son, they say he is
The best man that you have in your service.'
The king looks at him ferociously
And says: 'But that is lunacy!
What the devil makes you say that?
And who will be left to go ahead?'
'For that job,' replies Ganelon,
'Ogier of Denmark would be the best man.'

59   When count Roland hears that he
Has been proposed, he speaks sharply:
'Stepfather, why should I take it hard
That you choose me for the rear-guard?
Charlemagne won't be the loser.
Not a single horse or charger,
Not a mule, or a donkey even
Will be lost, if I am given
This command. All will be
Accounted for, without argument.

And my sword shall find out where it went.'
Ganelon says: 'I know that's true
And that is why I picked on you.'

60 When Roland hears that the rear-guard is
In fact to be his, he is furious.
He turns to his step-father angrily:
'What ancestors have you? Watch me!
I shall not let Charles's glove fall
As you did, before them all.'

61 'Great emperor,' says baron Roland,
'Give me the bow you have in your hand.
No one shall say I let it fall
As Ganelon did that stick.' And all
Watch the emperor, who does not raise
His head at all but only plays
With his beard and his moustaches
While tears collect on his eye-lashes.

62 Then Naimès came, no better man
In all the court; and he began:
'Sir, you have heard what has been said.
Count Roland is infuriated.
The rear-guard has fallen to his lot;
No baron can possibly alter that.
Give him the bow that you have bent
And let him have some competent
Men to help him.' It must be so.
The king gives, and Roland takes, the bow.

63 The emperor calls Roland: 'Nephew,
I shall leave half of my army with you.
Take them, you may need that many.'
The count says: 'I'd rather not have any!
God damn it, that would be a disgrace.
Give me twenty thousand French, I'll face

Whatever comes and you can go
Through the passes without a blow.'

64   Count Roland mounts upon his charger
And he is quickly joined by Oliver.
Then Gerin comes, and Gerer,
Otis and then Berengier;
Then Astor and old Anseïs
And Gerard of Roussillon, looking fierce;
Duke Gaifier comes, a powerful man.
The archbishop says: 'I'll go with Roland.'
'And I will too,' says Gautier.
'I've been with Roland till this day;
It is not for me to let him down.'
So twenty thousand join the count.

65   Roland calls Gautier de l'Hum.
'Take with you a thousand men,
Frenchmen of France, and keep an eye
On the narrow defiles and on the high
Places above them. The emperor
Must be protected as never before.'
Gautier says: 'I know my job.'
With a thousand Frenchmen he is off
To guard the defiles and the ridges.
He won't come back whatever the news is
Until his men have drawn their swords
And used them on the Saracen hordes.
King Almariz of Balferné
Is going to attack that very day.

66   The mountains are high, the valleys in shadow,
The passes sinister and rocks sallow.
For the French the day passes menacingly.
Their clatter and cries heard plain as can be
Fifty miles off. And when they come down
Into the old country, and they are on ground

Belonging to their lord, in Gascony,
Then they remember their own territories,
Think of their girls, of their noble ladies:
There is not one of them does not shed tears.
Charles thinks of those others, not without fear:
He has left his nephew in the passes of Spain.
He cannot, for pity, help weeping again.

67 They are left in Spain, the twelve peers,
With twenty thousand French who fear
Nothing, not death itself. The king
Is going back to France, hiding
His anguish under his heavy cloak.
It was the duke Naimès who spoke:
'Something is on your mind. What is it?'
Charles answers: 'A bad business.
Don't ask me. Well, it's Ganelon,
He'll be the end of France, that man.
Last night I had a dream;
He broke my spear to pieces, it seemed,
While I was holding it:
And it was he who played that trick
Of naming Roland for the rear-guard.
There he is now and it is hard
To know what the end of it will be.
God, he is irreplaceable for me!'

68 There are tears in Charlemagne's eyes.
A hundred thousand Frenchmen sigh
When they know of it; they fear
What may happen to Roland. They hear
Rumours of Ganelon's treason; the things
He accepted from the pagan king;
Gold and silver, silk and satin,
Mules and horses, and some add
Camels and lions. Marsilie
Meanwhile collects a huge army,

Summons counts, viscounts, almazors,
Dukes and emirs and many more,
All the young nobility
Of Spain, so many that in three
Days four hundred thousand men
Are brought together. Loudly then
In Saragossa they beat the drums.
Mahomet's image is lifted up
To the highest tower, and the pagans adore.
Prayer done, they make forced
Marches through the valleys and hills
Of the Certain Land, riding until
They see ahead the banners of France.
The rear-guard has not seen the advance
But the twelve peers will not refuse
The chance of battle, when they do.

69   Marsilie's nephew whacks his mule
And comes forward. With a broad smile
He says to his uncle: 'You'll agree
That you have had fair service from me.
I've put up with anything, always sought
After battles and won as many as fought.
Now give me the chance to have first crack
At Roland, I'll stop him dead in his tracks.
If Mahomet is with me, I will rid
Spain of the French for as long as I shall live,
From the passes right to Durestant.
Charles will have enough, all the Franks
Will cry for mercy. There's no other way
For you to have peace for the rest of your days.'
Thereupon king Marsilie moves
A pace and gives his nephew the glove.

70   Marsilie's nephew holds the glove tight
And when he speaks he is full of pride:
'Thank you, uncle, for what you have done.

Now choose me a dozen of your barons
And I will fight with the twelve peers.'
Falsaron is the first man there
To speak; he is Marsilie's brother:
'Nephew, we two will go together.
We'll let them have a battle all right
And if the rear-guard choose to fight
They'll have a chance to show their mettle.
We will kill the lot of them. That's settled.'

71   King Corsalis the necromancer,
From Barbary, is the next who advances:
He is no coward, he wouldn't have sold
Himself, not for all the gold
. . . . .
Malprimis de Brigant then appears,
A man who can keep up with a horse;
He speaks to the king at the top of his voice:
'I'll take myself to Roncevaux;
If I find Roland, that's all he'll know.'

72   There is an emir from Belaguer,
Of good appearance and gentle manner;
When he is once in the saddle his bearing
Is as proud as the armour he is wearing;
He passes for an excellent knight
And, were he a Christian, that would be right.
Before Marsilie he cries out:
'We'll see what Roncevaux is about!
If I find Roland, then he dies,
Oliver and the peers likewise.
The French will come to a bad end.
Charlemagne is aged and
Past his best. We'll get rid of the Franks.'
Marsilie gives the emir thanks.

73   An almazor from Moriane,
      The biggest rascal in all Spain,
      Starts boasting in front of the king:
      'Yes I and my lot will be going
      To Roncevaux, twenty thousand men
      —Just those with shields and lances, I mean.
      If I find Roland, he will fall:
      Charles will mourn him, but that's all.

74   Turgis of Tortelose comes; he
      Is a count and Tortelose his city.
      He never has a good word for Christians.
      He offers Marsilie his assistance:
      'Nothing to be afraid of! Mahomet
      Is a better man than Peter, their prophet.
      If you serve him we shall win the day.
      I'll find what Roland has to say
      At Roncevaux. You see my sword,
      A good long one. I give my word
      I'll try it out on Durandal;
      If anyone can do it, I shall.
      The French are finished if they try
      To hold against us. Charles will sigh
      And be sorry he ever came to Spain
      But he won't put on his crown again.'

75   Then comes Escrimiz—a gentleman
      From Valterne, and a Saracen.
      He calls to Marsilie from the crowd:
      'We'll soon see who looks so proud
      At Roncevaux. If Roland's there
      And I find him, let him beware;
      He'll go away without his head,
      Oliver too, who has always led
      The rest. And as sure as eggs are eggs
      The twelve peers won't stay on their legs.

So much for the French. France will be bled white
And Charles will find himself short of knights.'

76   There comes a pagan, Esturgant
With Estramaris—a pair of felons
And double-dealers, if ever there were.
Marsilie says: 'You are welcome here:
There's room for you at Roncevaux;
We need a few more to help with the show.'
'Nobody keener than us,' they answer,
'We'll pitch into Roland and Oliver
And all twelve peers will be left dead.
Our swords have an excellent cutting edge;
All they need is a little red.
The French will die, Charles be unhappy,
We'll make you a present of their Old Country.
Come and see us with your own eyes;
We'll give you the emperor if you like.'

77   Margariz of Seville comes running,
A man of great lands and plenty of money,
So handsome, all women are his friends;
They smile when they see him—can't help it—and
No pagan is a better knight.
He comes through the crowd and, to their delight,
Calls in a voice that drowns the rest:
'There is no occasion to be distressed;
At Roncevaux I shall kill Roland,
Oliver too, if he is at hand.
The twelve peers will be massacred.
Look at my sword, you may have heard
It was given me by the emir of Prime:
It will be bloody in no time.
The French will die, France will be dishonoured.
And old Charles with his lovely beard
Will sing a different sort of song.
We'll be all over France before long;

If you like, you can sleep in Saint-Denis.'
The king is pleased, and has reason to be.

78   Chernuble de Munigre comes then;
His hair sweeps on the ground. This man,
In sport, can carry more weight
Than four mules when they are loaded with freight.
In his land, so they say, the sun
Never shines, corn will not ripen,
No rains fall, there is no dew,
No stone that is not black. Some few
Travellers report that devils live there.
Now this Chernuble says: 'My sword
Is buckled on and I give my word
That at Roncevaux it will soon be red.
If I find Roland, I'll have his head,
Or call me a liar whatever I say.
Durandal will not stand in my way.
The French will die and France will be empty.'
All the twelve Saracen peers agree
With these words, and they draw close
To one another, while the whole host,
A hundred thousand of them, jostle round.
They go to arm upon pine-shaded ground.

79   The pagans arm, Saracen hauberks,
Most of them with three-ply steel-work.
They lace their helmets, Saragossan,
Buckle their swords on, many of them
Come from Vienna. They have good shields,
Valencian spears. They are ready for the field;
Their banners show white and blue and red.
Leaving the mules and hacks they're mounted
On chargers, and now they are riding
Stirrup to stirrup. The sun is shining,
A brilliant day, the armour reflects it.
A thousand trumpets sound to perfect it.

So great is the racket, the French hear.
Oliver says: 'The Saracens, I swear!
Now we are in it together.' 'Good!'
Roland replies, 'I hope to God!
We have to put up with heat and cold;
My lord, if he wishes, can have my scalp!
Let us make sure that none can say
We did not do our best this day.
Pagans are wrong and Christians right.
No one shall say I would not fight.'

80   Oliver climbs up to a ridge.
To his right, in a grassy valley is
The pagan army, coming his way.
He calls down to Roland: 'Hey!
On the Spanish side they are visible,
White hauberks, helmets flashing as well.
The French are in deep trouble now.
Ganelon knew. Remember how
He put our names to the emperor?
No question, that man is a traitor.'
Roland says: 'Quiet! Oliver,
Remember he's my step-father.'

81   Oliver, high up, looks again,
Far into the kingdom of Spain;
There are Saracens, so many of them!
Their helmets glitter with gold and gems;
He sees their shields, their burnished armour,
Their lances with the floating banners.
How many columns? He cannot count,
There are too many. He hurries down
The mountain-side like a man in a dream
And tells the French what he has seen.

82   Oliver says: 'I have seen more
Pagans than anyone ever before!

There must be a hundred thousand shields,
Laced helmets and hauberks in the field;
Spears at the ready, gleaming. If
You wanted battle, this is it.
All the strength God ever gave you
Is needed now, if he is to save you!'
The French say: 'What d'you think we are?
No one will run away from here.'

83 Oliver says: 'The pagans are on strength;
It seems to me there are very few French!
Roland, companion, you must sound your horn;
Charles will hear it, the army will return.'
Roland says: 'I'd miss my chance
And lose my reputation in France.
I shall do good work with Durandal,
It will be bloody up to the gold.
The pagan murderers came to the passes;
Now they will have to face their losses.'

84 'Companion, Roland, you must sound that horn
And Charles will tell the army to return.
The king and his troops will see us out of this.'
'For God's sake,' Roland answers, 'Miss
A chance and have my family blamed?
The whole of France would be ashamed!
It is not for nothing that I ride
With my sword Durandal at my side.
You'll see the blade covered in blood.
The pagans are as good as dead.'

85 'Sound your horn, Roland, companion:
Charles will hear it in the mountains.
I promise you, the French will come.'
'God forbid!' Roland answers, 'I'm
Not having anyone say to me
That I whistled for help. My family

Would just become a laughing-stock.
I'm not afraid of a few knocks.
I shall give plenty back. There will
Be plenty of blood on Durandal.
The French are all right, they will fight.
There won't be a Spaniard left by tonight.'

86   Oliver says: 'You won't be blamed.
I've seen these Saracens from Spain;
They are all over the valleys and
The lower slopes just here at hand.
The enemy is numerous
And there are only a few of us.'
Roland replies: 'So much the better.
God and his angels forbid I should let
France suffer dishonour this day!
Better die than any should say
I did not play my part as I should
Or make the emperor's claims good.'

87   Roland has pride and Oliver
Has sense; and both are without fear;
Once on their horses and in arms
They are indifferent to alarms.
They speak their minds like gentlemen.
They see the advancing Saracens.
Oliver says: 'Now, Roland, look,
They're near enough—and they have the luck
To know that Charles is miles away.
Yet you can't sound that horn, you say.
If the king were here, all would be safe.
Now take a look at the road from Spain.
There is the rear-guard. None of these men
Will ever do the king service again.'
Roland replies: 'That is absurd!
We shall hold our ground and push them back
And then we will go in and attack.'

88   Roland sees the battle is on:
      He is as proud as leopard or lion.
      He calls the French, and Oliver:
      'No more talk of how many they are!
      The emperor left us the French,
      The pick of them. He knew our strength,
      He knew there are no cowards here.
      We know what we have to endure,
      Bitter cold and blazing heat,
      And if we have to bleed, we bleed.
      You have spears, I have Durandal,
      My sword the king presented. Small
      Matter if I die. The next owner can
      Say it belonged to a good man.'

89   Then comes Turpin, the archbishop.
      He spurs his horse to a hill-top,
      Calls the French and preaches a sermon:
      'Charles has left us here, lord barons.
      He is the king. It is our duty
      To die for him and Christianity.
      It's battle now for all you men;
      There they are, the Saracens!
      Confess your sins, and God's forgiveness
      Will be ensured for those I bless.
      If you die, you will be, as martyrs,
      High in Paradise hereafter.'
      The French respond to this appeal;
      Instantly they dismount and kneel.
      The archbishop blesses them. The penance
      He enjoins is, to fight for France.

90   The French get on their feet again;
      They are absolved, their sins have gone:
      The archbishop, in the name of God,
      Has signed them with the sign of the cross.
      They mount their chargers rapidly

And are equipped as knights should be,
All ready and in battle order.
Count Roland says to Oliver:
'You were right enough to say, old son,
We'd been betrayed by Ganelon;
He has taken gold and goods and money;
He didn't get all that for nothing.
I only hope the emperor
Gives him his due and then some more.
Marsilie's paid for us, I suspect
He won't find it so easy to collect.'

91   Roland rides through the Spanish pass
On his horse Veillantif. He has
His armour on and looks well in it,
The point of his spear with the sun on it
Held up, with its white banner high
And fringes flapping against his side.
A noble figure, an open face,
Laughing. Following in second place
Is Oliver. The French acclaim
Their leader, who looks with disdain
Upon the Saracens, but gently,
Humbly even, upon the Frenchmen,
Whom he addresses courteously:
'My lords and barons, softly! Walk!
The pagans now are really caught;
They come here to be massacred.
Before night they will have been well served
And the king of France be richer than ever.'
With that, the armies come together.

92   Oliver says: 'No point now
In talking. You would not blow
Your horn, you haven't got the king.
It's not his fault; he knows nothing;
Nor is it the fault of your knights.

Ride on now; we have to fight.
My lords, barons, do your best;
I pray God that you will not rest
Till the job is finished. Let us hear
Charles's war-cry loud and clear!'
The French respond with a great shout:
'Mountjoy!' No one who heard it could doubt
This was an army in good heart.
They spur their horses and make a charge
And proud they look as they go in
To hit the enemy and win.
But the Saracens are waiting for
Them. They too understand war.

93   Marsilie's nephew, called Aelroth,
Rode in front of the Saracen host.
He had no good to say of the French:
'You murderers, where are your friends?
Your king has let you down, he was
Mad to leave you here in the pass.
Today will see France spat upon
And Charles will lose his right-hand man.'
Roland hears these words with sorrow.
He digs in his spurs and lets his horse go
And throws his whole weight at the count
Who is sent reeling to the ground;
His shield is smashed, his hauberk ripped,
His spine is bent, you can see his ribs;
His soul has gone and Roland's spear
Is so deep in that he appears
To brandish the corpse before it falls
With the neck broken. Then Roland calls:
'You rascal! Our king let no one down.
He knew that we should hold our ground
And that we should win honour here.
And that France would not be the loser.

Frenchmen, God will make us strong!
We are in the right, those thieves in the wrong.'

94   There is a duke called Falsaron,
Marsilie's brother; Abiron
And Dathan are his territory;
There is no bigger rascal than he.
His face and forehead are so wide
There is six inches between his eyes.
Furious to see his nephew dead,
He pushes out, gives his horse his head,
Uttering the pagan battle-shout,
And adds insulting words about
Their lovely France losing her honour.
His words are heard by Oliver
Who, in resentment, spurs his horse
And rides at him with all the force
He can, smashes his shield and rips
His hauberk, and driving some strips
Of pennon in his body; so
Out of the saddle the corpse goes.
Oliver looks at it, and says:
'You rascal, so much for your threats!
Come on the French, more of them must die!'
And shouts 'Mountjoy!' the emperor's battle-cry.

95   There is a king called Corsablix
From Barbary, across the seas;
He calls the other Saracens:
This is our battle, we have the men,
The French are few, nothing to fear
From the poor handful who are here.
Charles will not save a single man;
If we want to finish them, we can.'
Archbishop Turpin heard this boast
From one he hated more than most.
His golden spurs touch his horse's sides
And with great courage, off he rides.

He smashes the Saracen's shield, his spear
Goes through hauberk and midriff and re-appears
On the other side. He heaves the body
And it falls to the ground, heavily.
He looks down at the rascal and says:
'You lying pagan, Charles will save
Us. He has never let us down
And Frenchmen always stand their ground.
It is your troops that will crack up
And we shall make them do so. But
The news for you is, you are dead.'
Then, looking up: 'Come on the French!
Thank God that one of them has gone!'
He cries 'Mountjoy!' to show who won.

96   The shield of Malprimis de Brigal
Proves to be worth nothing at all
When Gerin charges at him. The boss
Splits at once and half is lost.
Gerin runs his spear right through
His hauberk and his body too.
Like a sack of flour the pagan falls
And Satan carries off his soul.

97   Then Gerer charges at the emir,
Smashes his shield, rips pieces of armour
Off his hauberk, then he puts
His spear right into the man's guts,
Carries him on it and throws him down.
Oliver says: 'We are gaining ground!'

98   Duke Samson, next in the field,
Charges and smashes the almazor's shield
With all its pretty flowers and gold.
The pagan's armour does not hold
And Samson's spear goes through his heart,
Liver and lungs and he falls hard.

He is not worth a lot of tears;
The archbishop Turpin watches and admires.

99   Then Anseïs spurs his horse and goes
Fast at Turgis of Tortelose,
Smashes his shield with its gilded boss,
Splits his double armour across
And sends the spear into his body,
Pushing it through till he can see
The steel tip at the other side,
Then lifts him up and throws him wide.
Roland loves such dexterities.
'That's the way to do it,' he says.

100   Engelier, Gascon, of Bordeaux,
Spurs his horse and lets it go.
Escrimiz de Valterne is his
Target and he damages
His shield so that it falls in splinters;
His spear goes through his hauberk and enters
His heart below the collar bone.
Then the pagan is lifted and thrown
Dead from the saddle. Engelier yells:
'That is another one in hell!'

101   Then Oton charges at a pagan,
And there goes the shield of Estorgan,
The white and red quarters in bits;
The skirts of his hauberk split;
The spear goes straight into his body.
The pagan's horse runs on; he drops.
Then Oton looks at him and says: 'Who
Do you suppose is saving you?'

102   Bérengier charges Altramariz,
Smashing his shield; his spear passes
Through the hauberk and into the flesh.

A thousand Saracens hold their breath.
That accounts for ten of the
Twelve Saracen peers, which leaves
Two to go and they are these:
Chernubles and Margariz.

103   Margariz is very tough,
Quick-moving, strong; handsome enough.
He charges at Oliver,
His spear smashes the shield under
The golden boss, and glances past
Oliver's ribs, then the shaft
Is broken, under God's protection.
Oliver is not hurt, the pagan
Rides on unimpeded and then
Sounds his trumpet to rally his men.

104   The battle becomes a free-for-all.
Roland takes no precautions at all,
He plies his spear until it breaks,
Fifteen assaults is what it takes.
Then he draws Durandal, his sword,
Charges Chernubles, spurring his horse;
Smashes the helmet with the gems;
Slices the skull, slices between
The eyes, halving the face, then cutting
The white hauberk as if it were nothing
And the whole body down to the fork,
Through the saddle with the goldsmith's work
He reaches the horse and splits his spine.
The horse and man at the same time
Are thrown on the grass. Oliver
Addresses the corpse: 'Ah, murderer!
Mahomet will not help you now.
Battles aren't won by rascals like you.'

105   Count Roland rode across the ground,
       Slashing and slicing all around,
       Saracen after Saracen flayed.
       You should have seen what carnage he made:
       Blood everywhere, there were pools of it!
       Blood on his hauberk, his arms dripped,
       His horse bloody up to the withers.
       Nor was Oliver backward either.
       Of none of the twelve peers could it be said
       He didn't add to the pile of dead.
       The French laid blows on thick and fast;
       Pagans died or were left gasping.
       The archbishop blessed the barons and shouted
       The emperor's battle-cry, Mountjoy!

106   Oliver rides through the thick
       Of the battle, he has only a stick
       Left in his hand, his lance is broken
       But still he charges at the pagan
       Malon, smashes his fancy shield,
       Makes his eye jump out of his head
       And leave his brains all over his boots
       And him dead with the rest of the brutes.
       Then he kills Turgis and Esturgoz
       And once again his lance broke off.
       Roland says: 'Hey, what are you up to?
       I'd not use that if I were you,
       Better to use a bit of steel,
       Something that people can really feel.
       Where's your sword? It's not just there
       For its jewelled pommel, your Hauteclaire!'
       'I couldn't draw it,' said Oliver.
       'No time, one way and another.'

107   With that Oliver drew his sword
       As if responding to Roland's words,
       And shows he can make use of it.

Justin de Val Ferrée is hit,
His head is sliced right down the middle,
Body and byrny down to the saddle,
And finally the horse's spine.
Down they go. Roland says: 'That's fine!
That's what the emperor likes to see!'
There are shouts of 'Mountjoy!' from half the army.

108 Count Gerin on his horse Sorel,
Gerer on Passecerf, do well.
They let their horses go, and ride
At Timozel, deep in the pagan side;
One strikes his shield and one his byrny
And both run him through the body
And there he is dead on the ground.
It was a race, which of them won
I cannot say. And Siglorel
Was killed by the archbishop. Hell
Was nothing new for the enchanter,
He had been there with Jupiter.
Turpin said: 'He was meant for me!'
Roland replied: 'The rascally
Wizard has caught it this time. Here,
Did you see that one, Oliver?'

109 The battle has become ferocious,
The blows on both sides marvellous,
Some in attack, some in defence.
So many spear-shafts broken and bent,
So many pennons and banners down,
So much blood everywhere around!
So much loss of young French lives!
They won't see their mothers or wives
Nor their friends waiting back in France.
Charlemagne weeps, but he has no chance
Of coming to rescue them. They are gone.
What a day's work for Ganelon

Who went to Saragossa to sell
His friends and struck the bargain so well!
He did less well in another place
For later he was hung in Aix
With thirty of his family
Who didn't know they had come to die.

110   The battle is intolerable.
Roland and Oliver fight well.
The archbishop strikes a thousand blows,
And the twelve peers are not slow;
All the French battle strenuously.
Hundreds and thousands of pagans die:
It's either death or running away
And there is no escape that day.
The French lose the best they have, these men
Will not see father or home again,
Nor Charlemagne waiting at the pass.
In France, at the same hour, there was
Terrible storm, thunder and wind,
Rain and hail; lightning skimmed
The country-side. There was earthquake
From *de periculo* to the Saints,
From the port of Wissant to Besançon,
Not a house but had a wall cave in.
It is dark at midday, the only light
Is when heaven splits and a bolt strikes.
No one sees but he is afraid.
'It is the end of time,' they say.
They don't know, don't understand
It is grief for the death of Roland.

111   The French have fought with all their heart,
The pagans too have done their part
And there are thousands of them dead;
Of their ten thousand, two are left.
The archbishop says: 'Our men are good,

No one on earth has better, or could have.
It is written by the Chroniclers,
He had the best, our emperor.'
They wander over the fields, looking
Each for his friends and kin, and weeping;
And yet the battle is not done:
Marsilie and his army come.

112   Marsilie comes along a valley
Accompanied by his huge army.
There are twenty columns with
Helmets glittering, and there is
Glitter too from shields and armour.
Seven thousand trumpets make a clamour
Through all the country round about.
Roland says: 'This leaves no doubt,
Oliver, we are betrayed.
Ganelon surely was not paid
For nothing, and we are to die:
The emperor will ask him why.
We shall have such a battle here
As never was. What does it matter?
I'll strike some blows with Durandal
And you with Hauteclaire. Think all
The places we have carried them in,
Used them to good effect to win
So many battles! None shall say
They had no edge on them today.'

113   Marsilie sees what massacre
Of heathen there has been. He orders
Trumpets to sound throughout the army.
He himself rides with the main body;
In front, Abisme, a Saracen,
A traitor and the worst of men.
He does not believe in God, and Mary
To him is nothing but a story:

He is black as melted pitch, and more
Fond of murder than even of gold.
No one ever saw him laugh.
He is violent and rash
And therefore loved by Marsilie.
He bears the dragon-flag, and proudly,
The archbishop hates him; when he knows
He is there, he wants to come to blows.
He mutters: 'That man makes me sick.
He's an outrageous heretic;
The best thing I could do is kill
Him, I've got some courage still.'

114 And so the battle is begun
By the archbishop. His horse is one
He took from Grossaile, who was a king
He killed in Denmark—a fast-running
Animal, well-breathed, neat-footed,
With fine legs and broad rump, well suited
To the work he has to do;
His tail is white, his mane yellow,
With little ears and tawny head;
Runs like a greyhound, it is said.
The archbishop, being the man he is
Digs his spurs in hard and charges;
Nothing will stop him getting Abisme.
The shield is shattered as in a dream
With all its topazes and diamonds.
Galafé had it from a demon
In Val Metas, but for all that
It is worth nothing when Turpin strikes it.
He slices Abisme from side to side
And that is how that Saracen died.
The French say: 'The archbishop, look!
Has the right hands to hold a crook!'

115   Pagans are so numerous
        Everywhere, the French are anxious.
        They grumble. Oliver and Roland,
        And the twelve peers, are they at hand?
        The archbishop thereupon speaks his mind:
        'What has come over you, are you blind?
        I hope to God you are not thinking
        Of making off. A fine thing!
        People will make up songs about you.
        Better to die fighting. The end
        Cannot be far away, my friends.
        We shall not live beyond today,
        But one thing I can certainly say:
        Heaven will open its doors as wide
        As when the Holy Innocents died.'
        That cheers them up, and they annoy
        The enemy by shouting 'Mountjoy'.

116   A Saracen is there who owns
        Half of Saragossa town:
        Climorin—not a good man.
        He is that friend of Ganelon
        Who, after the latter's oath,
        Smiled and kissed him on the mouth,
        Gave him his jewelled helmet too.
        He now talks big about what he'll do
        To the old country: slap her down
        And rob the emperor of his crown.
        His horse Barbamousche will go
        Faster than any hawk or swallow.
        He spurs it on, leaves the rein free
        And charges Engelier of Gascony
        Whose shield and byrny come apart
        So that the spear reaches his heart
        And passes through, and he is thrown
        On the ground like a bag of stones.
        The pagan shouts: 'That's all they're fit

For; come on, thin them out a bit!'
The French exclaim: 'Oh, God!' and then:
'We can't afford all these good men.'

117   Count Roland calls to Oliver:
'Now we have lost Engelier.
We had no better man than he.'
The count replies: 'Leave it to me.'
He jabs the golden spur in and
Holds Hauteclaire, bloody, in his hand,
Charges and strikes with all his force.
The Saracen tumbles off his horse
And devils carry off his soul.
Oliver wastes no time at all;
He leaves the duke Alphaien dead
And cuts off Escababi's head,
Unseating seven Arabs besides
—They're useless when they've nothing to ride.
Roland says: 'He has lost his temper!
Oh, he's worth his keep, Oliver.
Charles loves to see us fight like that.'
Then louder: 'You knights, throw them back!'

118   Then comes the pagan Valdabron,
Long at Marsilie's disposition.
He has a fleet, four hundred galleys
And is the master of the seas.
He took Jerusalem by treason
And smashed the temple of Solomon,
Killing the patriarch at the font.
After the traitor Ganelon
Swore his oath, he gave him his sword
With quantities of jewels and gold.
He rides a horse called Gramimond
Who is as swift as any falcon.
His spurs are sharp, he digs them in
And charges at the great duke Samson,

Smashes his shield, rips his hauberk
And puts the pennon through his shirt,
Right through his body, and strikes him down
Out of the saddle, dead on the ground. . . .
'Come on the pagans! We shall win!'
The French say: 'Bad that we've lost him!'

119   When Roland sees Samson is dead,
Furious, he gives his horse his head;
Spurring, he charges at the pagan.
He brandishes Durandal again,
The sword that's worth its weight in gold,
Strikes the jewelled helmet, with all
The strength he has, splits it, the head,
Byrny, body, and saddle. The dead
Man falls, the horse's back is broken.
The pagans looking on are shaken.
Roland says: 'You're a gang of outlaws!
You lot are fighting in the wrong cause!'

120   Then there came an African
From Africa, called Malquiant,
The son of king Malcud; with gold
All over him, he shows up. He calls
His horse Saut-Perdu; it can race
Any horse in any place.
He charges at Anseïs's shield,
Leaves red and blue fragments in the field;
Rips the skirt of his hauberk and puts
His spear through his body, up to the wood.
The count is dead, his time is done.
The French say: 'We shall miss that one!'

121   Then comes Turpin, the archbishop.
Never was there another such
Tonsured man who could say mass
Yet perform acts of such prowess.

He says to the pagan: 'God damn you! You
Have killed one I am sorry to lose.'
He throws his horse across the field
And smashes the Toledo shield,
Throwing its owner dead on the grass . . .
. . . . .

122   Then there is Grandoine, who is son
To Capuel, the Cappadocian
King. Marmoire, his horse, is faster
Than any bird. And now he dashes,
Rein slack, spurs working, at Gerin,
Smashes his red shield, pushes in
His spear, then carrying his blue
Flag through byrny and body too,
Throws him dead on a high rock.
He kills Gerer and then cuts off
Bérengier and Guy St Anthony.
And charges the great duke Austorge
Of Valence and Envers on the Rhône
And strikes him dead with a single blow.
The pagans are delighted but
The French say: 'We are losing a lot!'

123   Hearing his men's discouraged words
Count Roland grips his bloody sword;
He feels as if his heart would break.
He says to the pagan: 'It will take
More than you think to pay for those!'
He spurs his horse and off he goes.
They are well-matched, you might ask whether
Roland will win. They come together.

124   Grandoine was courageous, strong,
With plenty of fight. It isn't long
Before he finds Roland across his
Path. He easily recognises

The count, though he hasn't seen him before:
The proud features, the fine build, and still more
The look and carriage are such that he
Cannot help feeling fear when he sees.
He wants to get away, but can't
Because of the blow struck by the count
Which splits his helmet to the nose-piece,
Divides his nose, his mouth, his teeth,
All his body, hauberk and mail
And the horse's back down to the tail
And the saddle with its silver points.
They are dead; there is no rejoinder.
The Spanish side lets out a groan.
The French say: 'We still have Roland.'

125   The battle gathers speed, the French
Strike fiercely and with all their strength,
The cut up knuckles, ribs and spines,
The garments and the flesh behind;
On the green grass the blood flows . . .
  . . . . .
'Mahomet curses your Old Country,
Your people and their bravery!'
Not one Saracen but is soon calling
For help from Marsilie, their king.

126   The battle is unmerciful,
The French spears strike, the Saracens fall.
Never was such a grim proceeding,
So many dead, wounded and bleeding!
Some on their backs, some on their faces;
The Saracens cannot stand the pace;
They are shaken and irresolute.
They retreat. The French go in pursuit.

127   Count Roland calls to Oliver:
'You must admit, my old partner,

The archbishop does extremely well,
There isn't a better man anywhere;
Yes, he knows how to handle a spear!'
The count replies: 'Let's help him then!'
At that the French begin again.
There is a sharp exchange of blows,
The Christians are in trouble now.
Roland and Oliver cut and thrust;
Their swords won't collect any rust.
The archbishop uses his spear.
How many men met their end here
Is written in the chronicles,
The *Gesta* says four thousand, no less.
They manage well in four attacks
But the fifth they cannot throw back:
All the French soldiers have been killed
Except for sixty, by God's will;
These will die too, but before they do
They will exact a life or two.

128   Roland looks at his dead, considers
The scene, and appeals to Oliver:
'What do you think, for God's sake? There are
So many good men lying there!
Hard luck on France, our poor old country,
With this place like a cemetery!
And where's the king, why's he not here?
How can we manage, Oliver?
How can we get news to him now?'
Oliver says: 'I don't know how.
All I know is, it's better to die
Than to suffer infamy.'

129   Roland says: 'I will sound the horn.
Charles will hear it and will return.
The Franks will come back through the pass.'
Oliver says: 'It would bring disgrace

On you and upon all your kin:
All their lives they would hear of it!
When I told you to blow, you refused.
To do so now would be of no use
And you shall not do it with my consent;
It would not be the act of a friend.
Look, your arms are covered in blood!'
Roland says: 'Yes, I have done some good.'

130   Roland says: 'Things are getting tough;
I'll blow, Charles will hear soon enough.'
Oliver says: 'It's cowardice now!
When I asked you, you said no.
If we'd had the king, we'd have been all right.
It's not the fault of these dead knights.'
Oliver goes on: 'And, by God,
If ever I see my sister Aude,
You shall never lie in her arms!
You have already done enough harm.'

131   Roland says: 'Why get angry with me?'
Oliver: 'Your responsibility!
Courage can be reasonable;
Why must you behave like a fool?
Moderation is better than being
So rash you don't know what you're doing.
It's your stupidity killed those French!
A fat lot that does for Charles's strength!
If you'd listened to me, Charles would have come,
We would have fought the battle and won
And taken Marsilie alive or dead.
Oh, your prowess, Roland! Where has it led?
We're no use now to the emperor
And by God he deserves better!
There'll never be another like him.
You will die, and for France things are grim.

We have often fought together, you and I
And now, before evening, we must die!'

132   The archbishop hears the argument
And quickly gallops up to them:
'Roland!' Gently he remonstrates.
'And Oliver! Now for God's sake,
Try to settle your differences.
Sounding the horn will not save us,
But it might be the best thing to do;
The king can avenge us; he will want to.
The Spanish shouldn't go home happy!
If the French come here they will see
All our dead. They will dismount
And make a thorough search of the ground,
Put our bodies on stretchers, transport
Them to France, give them some sort
Of proper attention. We could do worse
Than see they are buried in a church
And not eaten by dogs and pigs.'
Roland replies: 'That's easy to fix.'

133   Roland takes the horn and grips
It tightly, presses it to his lips
And blows a blast with all his strength.
The mountains are high. Through them the French
Hear the sound thirty leagues away.
Charles hears it. What does he say?
'That means battle. Our men are there.'
Ganelon does not want to hear.
'Had another said that,' he replies,
'I should have said it was a lie.'

134   Roland, with immense effort,
Blows his horn until it hurts.
The blood trickles from his lips,
The veins in his forehead split.

The sound carries far and wide.
Charles hears it as he rides.
Duke Naimès hears it, the Franks hear.
The king says: 'Roland's horn! He'd never
Sound it, if it weren't in a fight.'
Ganelon answers: 'He well might!
You're too old, and that's a fact;
It's childishness to talk like that.
You know how proud Roland is;
I'm surprised God put up with him.
He took Noplès without orders;
Out came the Saracen marauders.
He had his fight, then had to flood
The field, it was so covered in blood.
He will sound his horn for little enough;
It is some game and he's showing off.
He'll do it all day for a hare.
Who would attack him? No one would dare!
Go on riding. We're not home yet.
Why do you stop then? Did you forget?'

135 Count Roland has his mouth bloody,
The veins have burst in his forehead;
He sounds the horn in extreme pain.
Charles hears, the French strain
To catch every reverberation.
The king says: 'How long it lasts!'
Naimès: 'A strong man blew that blast!
He has a battle on his hands;
He has been betrayed by the very man
Who now asks you to run away.
Arm yourself, raise your battle-cry!
Think of the people you have there!
You have heard Roland in despair.'

136 The emperor's trumpets sound the alarm.
The French dismount and quickly arm

With hauberks, helmets, brilliant swords.
They have magnificent shields, unflawed
Lances and spears, red, white and blue
Banners. Soon they are spurring through
The pass, the captains on chargers. They say:
'If we find Roland alive this day
We'll show him what we can do.' Maybe,
But for action you must arrive promptly.

137   Evening is coming, the day wears on,
Arms and armour reflect the sun.
Hauberk and helmets, flower-painted shields
Seem to throw flames across the field;
There is glitter from gilded flags and spears.
How sombrely the emperor
Rides! And the French with him, upset
And angry, they cannot forget
Roland, and the danger he is in.
'Seize Ganelon,' orders the king,
'And hand him to the kitchen boys.'
He calls the master cook, and says:
'Besgon, put him under guard.
He has betrayed my house.' There are
A hundred lads there to receive him,
The best and worst of them are pleased.
They pull hairs from his beard and moustache,
Each gives him four blows with his fist.
They beat him with sticks and cudgels, they get
A chain and put it round his neck
Then chain him up just like a bear.
They load him on a donkey, and so
They cosset and look after him
Till they have to give him back to the king.

138   The mountains are high and full of shadows,
The valleys deep, the streams rapid.
They sound the trumpets as they advance

To give Roland an answer from France.
The emperor rides sombrely,
The French are upset and angry;
Tears start from their eyes, they grieve
And pray to God that he will save
Roland until they reach the place
Where they can save France from disgrace.
What is the point of it? There is none,
The time for praying has already gone.

139   King Charles rides on in fury,
His white beard outside his byrny.
All the French barons use their spurs,
Not one of them but wishes he were
Already with Roland, their captain
When he is fighting the Saracens.
He is in trouble, cannot survive,
Possibly, till they arrive.
God, those sixty men he has
Are the best that any captain could have!

140   Roland looks at the mountainside
On which so many Frenchmen have died
And can no longer hold back his tears:
'God have mercy on you peers
And lords, and grant that in Paradise
You may lie among roses and lilies!
I never set eyes on better men.
So long have you served with me and conquered
So many lands for the emperor!
Was it for this he bred you up?
Ah, France, you are the sweetest country,
Now deserted, you may thank me.
French barons, I see you die
And cannot help you in any way.
God help you, he never lies.
Oliver, you are my brother, but I

Have failed you, and I shall die
Of grief, if not in another way.
Let us fight on and finish this day.'

141   Count Roland is back in the battle,
Laying about him with Durandal.
Faldrun de Pui is cut in two,
Twenty-four others sliced right through:
Never a man so wanted revenge
As Roland for his massacred French!
They run like deer before the dogs,
Those pagans escaping Roland's knocks!
The archbishop says: 'You are doing well;
So a man should do who is able
To bear arms and sit on a horse.
Courage should be a matter of course.
A man without is no good to me:
As well be a monk in a monastery,
Praying all day long for our sins!'
Roland replies: 'Come on, pitch in!'
With that the Franks set to again,
But it didn't go so well for the Christians.

142   When it is known that there will be
No prisoners, men fight desperately.
So with the French, who are like lions.
Marsilie, every inch a baron
Comes riding Gaignon, a fine horse.
He uses his spurs, and with all his force
Charges Bevon, who when at home
Is lord of Dijon and of Beaune.
He smashes his shield, goes through the hauberk
And this one blow completes the work.
Then he kills Yvoire and Ivon,
And with them Gerard of Roussillion.
Count Roland is not far away.
He says to the pagans: 'You will pay

For that, God damn you, they're my men!
Before you touch another of them
You'll find out what my sword is called!'
With that, a blow from Durandal
Which severs Marsilie's right hand.
After that the count Roland
Has off the head of Jurfaleu,
Marsilie's son. The pagans drew
Aside and prayed: 'Help us, Mahomet!
All our gods, help us, and let
Us be avenged on the emperor!
He has sent us a pack of murderers
Who would rather die than leave us in peace.'
They say to each other: 'No more great feats!'
A hundred thousand of them make tracks
For home; no one can call them back.

143   What's the good? If Marsilie's gone
His uncle Marganice has not:
Marganice of Carthage who
Rules in Ethiopia too
—A damned land. He is the leader
Of the big-nosed, flat-eared black people,
There are fifty thousand of them here.
They ride boldly, furiously,
Howling their pagan war-cry.
Roland says: 'We may be martyred
And anyhow shall soon be parted;
Let us at least sell ourselves dear.
You know how to use your swords here,
No easy life, no easy death
And honour France with your last breath!
When my lord Charles comes, let him find
Fifteen dead pagans to one man of mine,
Then he'll say we taught a lesson.
That way we shall be sure of his blessing.'

144   When Roland sees the cursed race
       Black as ink and whose faces
       Have nothing white except the teeth,
       He says: 'Now I know indeed
       That we shall die today. Pitch in!
       Come on the French! I will begin!'
       Oliver says: 'No hanging back!'
       With that the French ride to attack.

145   When the pagans see the French are few
       Their pride and confidence are renewed.
       They say: 'It is the emperor's
       Cause that is bad, it isn't ours!'
       Marganice, on his sorrel horse,
       Rides against Oliver at full force,
       Sticking his spear into his back;
       It comes out at the front. At that
       He says: 'Charlemagne left you to find
       A wound like that when he left you behind!
       He wronged the pagans, but this makes up
       For all the harm he did to us.'

146   Oliver knows his wound is mortal.
       He grips Hauteclaire, with its hard steel
       Strikes Marganice on his pointed helmet,
       Which splits in a shower of ornaments,
       And cuts his head to the front teeth.
       Marganice falls underneath
       His horse and Oliver says: 'Pagan!
       I don't say Charles hasn't lost a man
       But you will not go boasting now
       In what used to be your country, how
       You got the upper hand of me.
       You won't be talking to the ladies
       About me or about anyone!'
       Then he calls for Roland to come.

147   Oliver knows he is near his end.
How can he take enough revenge?
He hacks away in the thick of it,
He chops up shields and spears and ribs,
Backbones and saddles, feet and hands,
Throwing one Saracen so that he lands
On top of another. You would have said,
If you could have seen his heap of dead,
There was a fighting man to remember!
He does not forget Charles's war-cry either;
'Mountjoy!' he cries out loud and clear.
He calls Roland, his friend and peer:
'I have served you and served with you,' he says,
'Before night we must go our separate ways.'

148   Roland looks at Oliver's face
Which is pale, discoloured and greyish;
Blood runs down his body, clots
Form on the ground. Roland says: 'God!
I do not know what I shall do,
Old comrade, if I must lose you.
Never another such! Mischance
Today has fallen upon France;
Never has she been so distressed,
So many men! And those the best!
The emperor is the loser.' With that
He swoons there where he sits, on horseback.

149   There is Roland, swooning on his horse
And Oliver, who is half a corpse.
He has bled so much his eyes are troubled;
Far or near he can discover
Nothing clearly, recognises no man.
When he meets his old companion
He strikes him, splits his helmet in two
Down to the nose-piece—but not through
To the head, which is quite untouched.

Roland looks at him with much
Affection and says tranquilly:
'Surely that was not meant for me?
It is I, Roland, your old friend
Who wants only to make amends.'
Oliver says: 'Now I hear you speak.
I cannot see you, I am too weak.
May God see you. I am sorry,
When I struck you I struck blindly.'
Roland answers: 'No harm done,
And, before God, I wish you none.'
They bow to one another and so
Part with great love between the two.

150   Oliver knows he will soon be dead;
His eyes roll upwards in his head.
He can see nothing, hear no sound;
He dismounts and crouches on the ground.
Loudly he cries that he has sinned.
Holding towards heaven his two hands joined
Seeks Paradise with God's compliance.
He blesses Charlemagne and sweet France
And his friend Roland above all.
His heart fails and his helmet falls,
Then his whole body hugs the earth.
The count has spoken his last word.
The noble Roland mourns and weeps
As never man has ever grieved.

151   Roland sees his friend in death,
Face down and with dust in his teeth.
Very gently he says good-bye:
'Oliver, so there you lie!
We have been days and years together
And never either harmed the other;
With you dead, there is nothing in life.'
Still sitting upon Veillantif

The marquis faints, but he cannot fall,
Held upright by his stirrups of gold.

152 Before Roland comes to, and is
Recovered from his fainting fit,
Disaster comes, the French fall
So many, he has lost them all
Except only the archbishop
And Gautier de l'Hum, down from the top
Of the ridge, where he resisted
Till every man of his was dead;
Now he has no alternative
But to come down where Roland is
And ask for help. 'Where are you now,
My general?' he says to the count.
'I was never afraid when you were there.
It is Gautier, the conqueror
Of Maelgut, I the nephew of old
Droon with the white hair, you told
Me earlier you trusted me.
My spear is broken now, my shield
Holed, my coat of mail in pieces,
My body itself pierced. . . .
I shall die, but I can say
I have made the enemy pay.'
As he said that Roland heard
And rode towards him, using his spurs.

153 Roland is grieved and furious;
He pushes into the thick of it and slashes
The men of Spain, there are twenty less alive;
Gautier kills four, the archbishop five.
The pagans say: 'These men are murderers!
Make sure they don't get away from here!
Only traitors fail to attack,
Only cowards turn their backs!'

Then again the hue and cry,
They close upon them from all sides.

154   Count Roland is a noble soldier,
Gautier de l'Hum a fine performer,
The old archbishop is another;
Each wants not to fail the others.
They are all in the thick of it.
A thousand Saracens on foot,
Forty thousand mounted, but
Not one of them dares to go near.
They throw their lances and their spears,
Arrows, darts and javelins.
Gautier is killed at once, Turpin
Of Reims has his shield holed,
His helmet smashed, his head mauled,
His hauberk pierced, the mail gone
And four spears right through his body;
His horse is killed under him;
With the archbishop down, things are grim.

155   Turpin sees he is on the ground
But four spears will not keep him down.
Rapidly he gets to his feet,
Looks at Roland, runs to meet
Him and says: 'I am undefeated!
No surrender while I live!'
He draws Almace, his sword, and gives
More than a thousand thrusts and cuts.
Charles will see he didn't give up
When he sees around him four hundred,
Some wounded, some without heads,
Some of them stuck through the middle.
That is what one who was at the battle
Reports, it is all in the *Geste*:
The noble Gilles, whom God so blessed,

Wrote it down in the abbey at Laon;
That's what the story is based upon.

156   Count Roland fights courageously
But his body is hot and sweaty,
He has a terrible pain in his head;
When he blew the horn, his temples bled.
But is Charles coming? He wants to know,
So once again, but feebly, he blows.
The emperor stops, listens and says:
'Things are not going well with us!
If the horn sounds so weakly it is
Because Roland has not long to live.
We must ride fast or he will be gone!
Sound the trumpets—every one!'
Sixty thousand of them blow,
The mountains ring, the valleys echo.
The pagans don't laugh at what they hear,
They know that Charles will soon be there.

157   The pagans say: 'The emperor!
It's the French trumpets, do you hear?
If Charles comes, we shan't last long;
If Roland lives, the war goes on
And we shall lose our land in Spain.'
At that four hundred helmeted men
Who think themselves the best in battle
Push from the army and assemble.
Together they launch a fierce attack:
How can Roland throw them back?

158   Roland sees them and summons at length
His pride, his ardour and his strength.
He won't give up while he has breath.
He is mounted upon Veillantif.
Once more he tries the golden spurs,
Forcing his way among the attackers,

With him Turpin, the archbishop.
The pagans say: 'He must be stopped!
We have heard the French trumpets, their king,
The most powerful of all, is coming!'

159   Count Roland never loved a coward,
An ill-intentioned man, a braggart
Or any disaffected man.
He calls to the archbishop Turpin:
'Sir, you're on foot and I'm mounted;
I will stay here on your account,
We'll take what comes and stand together.
I will not leave you now, whatever
Happens: we'll see some pagans fall;
They can't do better than Durandal.'
The archbishop says: 'We'll go for them!
Charles will be here; we shall be avenged.'

160   The pagans say: 'We have no luck!
And this day has not brought us much!
We have lost our lords, lost our peers,
Now Charles returns, with us still here.
Listen! the clear trumpets of France!
Cries of Mountjoy! The French advance.
Count Roland is immensely proud
And will not yield to flesh and blood.
One throw, and we will let him be.'
They hurl darts, javelins, every
Kind of weapon in the field;
They make great holes in Roland's shield,
Rip his hauberk, the mail smashed,
But his body is untouched.
Yet Veillantif is badly wounded
In thirty places, and falls dead.
The pagans make off and give up.
Count Roland is once more on foot.

161   The pagans are in flight, angrily,
Making their way through Spanish country.
Count Roland cannot go in pursuit,
Veillantif's dead, he is on foot,
Like it or not. And so he stops
Where he can give help to the archbishop.
He unlaces the gold-trimmed helmet,
Takes off the hauberk, then he gets
Pieces of his gown and stops
His gaping wounds with the stuff.
Then he takes him in his arms
And lays him gently on the grass.
Softly Roland says: 'If you
Will give me leave now, I will go.
Our friends and comrades we held dear
Are dead. We cannot leave them there.
They must be found, identified,
And laid before you side by side.'
The archbishop says: 'Go, take your time.
The field is yours, thank God, and mine.'

162   Roland wanders through the field alone,
Searches the hill-sides up and down, . . .
Finds Gerin, Gerer his companion,
Finds Bérengier and finds Aton.
He finds Anseis and Samson
And old Gerard of Roussillon.
He lifts and takes them one by one,
Brings them where the archbishop is
And lays them in a row at his knees.
The archbishop cannot hold back his tears.
He lifts his hand and blesses the peers
And then says: 'A bitter end,
Lords, for you who were my friends.
May God keep your souls in peace,
Wrapped in flowers in Paradise.

Now my death comes with anguish, nor
Shall I again see the emperor.'

163   Roland renews his search, discovers
His companion, Oliver.
He embraces him and takes him up
And carries him back to the archbishop.
He lays him on a shield and then
Puts him down beside his friends.
The archbishop gives him absolution,
Making the sign of the cross. The two of them
Then grieve bitterly over him.
Roland says: 'Noble Oliver,
You were the son of the duke Renier
Who held the marches, Val de Runers.
For breaking lances, holing shields
And bringing arrogant men to heel
And helping good men with arms and counsel
What land bred one who did as well?'

164   When Roland sees his peers are dead
And Oliver, who so delighted
Him, he weeps tenderly.
The colour leaves his face, and he
Cannot stand, so great his grief:
He cannot help it, he is faint.
The archbishop says: 'Short time remains.'

165   When the archbishop sees that Roland
Has fainted, he grieves, the good man;
He reaches out and takes the horn.
In Roncevalles clear water runs,
He wants to fetch some for the count
But struggles feebly over the ground;
He lacks strength, he has lost so much blood
And cannot move his legs as he would.

His heart gives, he falls forward, breath
Comes heavily, for this is death.

166   Roland recovers from his faint,
Gets on his feet, but in great pain,
Looks up and down the hill-side, sees
On the green grass, beside the peers,
Another noble baron, it is
The archbishop who did God's service.
He makes confession, hands together
And prays God take him into heaven.
He is dead, Charles's soldier, Turpin
Who in great battles and good sermons
Stood up against the Saracens,
God grant his blessing to him. Amen.

167   Roland sees Turpin on the ground,
All his innards hanging out
And his brains oozing from his forehead;
Below his collar-bone, on his breast
His fine white hands hold in a cross.
Solemnly Roland laments his loss:
'I commend you, noble soldier
Of noble race, to heavenly Glory;
No man served God better than you.
Since the apostles there has been
No such prophet, either to keep
The law of God or draw men to it.
May your soul have easy exit
And suffer nothing on the way
But rest in Paradise today.'

168   Roland feels his own death is near,
His brains trickle from his ears.
He prays God for his friends and calls
Upon the angel Gabriel.
He takes the horn, like a brave man

And Durandal in the other hand.
He goes a little more than a bowshot
Towards Spain and finds an empty plot.
He climbs a hillock where is an arbour
And under it four blocks of marble.
He falls face down and lies there fainting
On the green grass for death is coming.

169   High the mountains, high the arbour
And brightly shine the blocks of marble.
Faint on the green grass Roland lies.
A Saracen, shamming death, descries
Him from a heap of dead
And lifts up his blood-plastered head.
The man gets to his feet and runs
To where Roland is; he is a tall man,
Well-built and strong. Pride in his prowess
Fills him with a fatal madness.
He seizes Roland, body and weapons
And calls out: 'Charles's nephew is beaten!
I'll take this sword to Arab lands!'
Half-conscious, the count understands.

170   Roland feels him take the sword,
He opens his eyes, with these words:
'I don't think you are one of the French!'
He grips the horn with all his strength,
Strikes at the helmet's precious stones
And breaks the steel, the head, the bones
So that the eyes start from the head
And at his feet the man falls dead.
He says: 'Coward, how did you dare
To lay hands on me, whether it were
Honourably or dishonourably?
Everyone will know it was folly.
Now see, the horn is broken,
The jewels and the gold have fallen.'

171 Roland feels he is losing his sight.
His colour has gone, his face is white.
He stands up despite his heavy limbs.
A dark stone is in front of him,
He strikes it ten times in fury;
The steel shrieks, but it remains steady,
It does not break, is not even marked.
The count says: 'Saint Mary be my guard!
Ah, Durandal, you are so good,
I can do nothing with you now if I would.
I have won so many battles and
Conquered, with you in my hand,
Territories for Charlemagne.
How will you fare with a worse man?
You can say a good man held you once;
There will never be such another in France.'

172 Roland strikes the block of sardonyx,
The steel screams but it does not split.
When he finds he cannot make a dent
Roland utters this lament:
'Ah, Durandal, you are fine and white
And, in the sun, reflect the light.
In the valley of Maurienne an angel
Counselled Charles he would do well
To give it to a count his captain:
So I had it from Charlemagne.
With it I won for him Anjou,
Brittany and the Maine too.
I won Poitou and Normandy,
I won Provence and Lombardy,
All the Romagna, Aquitaine,
Bavaria, Burgundy, Flanders, Puillane;
Constantinople, which owed allegiance;
Saxony was brought to obedience;
I won Scotland, I won Ireland,
And England the king kept in his own hands;

With Durandal I conquered more
Lands than any man before.
And all for Charles with the white beard.
I am in sorrow for this sword.
Better die than leave it in pagan hands;
Father, avert this shame from France.'

173   Roland strikes on a block of grey stone,
A huge piece of it is sliced down;
The sword shrieks, but does not break;
It bounces back towards heaven's gate.
When the count sees that nothing will serve
To damage it, he utters these words:
'Ah, Durandal, you are fine and holy!
Your pommel holds relics, and how many!
St Peter's tooth, St Basil's blood,
St Denis's hair and a piece of the hood
Of St Mary: it would not be right
For a pagan to take you into a fight.
You ought to be in Christian hands,
And may you never belong to a man
Who has a touch of cowardice.
With you I conquered many countries
Which Charles with the flowing beard now holds.
The emperor now has both power and gold.'

174   Count Roland feels the chill of death,
Already present in his head,
Sinking down to reach his heart.
He runs towards a pine, falls hard
Face downwards, where the grass is green.
He puts his sword and horn between
Himself and the ground, and turns his head
Towards the pagans, so that when he is dead
Charles and all his men will say:
'The count won, after all, today!'

He says confession, weak as he is
And offers his glove to God, for his sins.

175   Roland knows that his time is up.
Looking towards Spain, on a steep slope,
With one hand he beats his breast:
'God, I have sinned against your greatness
From the day I was born until this day
When I am brought low in this way.'
He offers his glove to God the King;
Angels come down from heaven to him.

176   Count Roland lies under a pine-tree,
His face towards the Spanish country.
Many matters he calls to mind:
The countries he has conquered; old times
In his sweet France; his noble race;
Charles, who reared him in his palace;
He cannot help it, he weeps and sighs.
With *mea culpa*, he asks God's mercy:
'God the Father, in whom is truth,
Who raised St Lazarus from death
And saved Daniel in the lion's den,
Save my soul now I am at my end
From all the errors of my life.'
He offers God his right-hand glove.
St Gabriel takes it from his hand.
He lets his head fall forward and
Rests it upon his arm. Hands together
He yields his soul to God the Father.
God sent his angel Cherubin too
And St Michael *de periculo*.
With Gabriel, as the count dies,
They take his soul to Paradise.

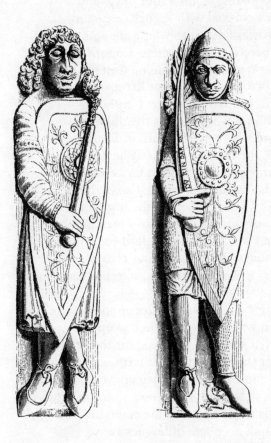

Statues of Roland and of Oliver in the portal of
Verona Cathedral (12th century)

177   Roland is dead, heaven has his soul.
The emperor reaches the Roncevalles.
There is no track anywhere around,
No pathway, not a foot of ground
Not covered with French or pagans.
Charles cries out, 'Where are you, Roland?
Where's the archbishop? Count Oliver?
Gerin and his companion Gerer?
Where is Oton? Count Bérengier?
Ivin and Ivoire, where, I say?
Anseïs? And where is the duke Samson
And where's old Gerard of Roussillon?
All the twelve peers I left here?'
No use calling, there is no answer.
'The battle is over, God!' says the king,
'Why wasn't I here at the beginning?'
He tugs at his beard like a man in fury
And weeps for all the dead French he sees.
Thousands of his men are dazed;
Duke Naimès, grieving, stares in amazement.

178   There is no knight or baron there
But weeps for pity. They weep for
Their sons and brothers, for their nephews,
For their friends, their lords, and not a few
Become insensible, they grieve so.
Duke Naimès, the wisest, is not so slow;
It is he who says to the emperor:
'Look, a couple of leagues away,
The dust rising from the highway,
That means there are pagans there!
Ride on! Avenge this horror!'
'Ah, God!' says Charles, 'what a distance!
What is best for the honour of France?
They have taken all the flower of my men.'
The king orders Gebuin and Oton,
Tibbald of Reims and Milon the count:

'Guard the field, the valleys, the mountains
And let the dead stay where they are.
Let no animal touch them, nor
Any squire or boy go near;
No one at all till we're back here.'
'We'll see to it,' they answer gently
And take a thousand men for this duty.

179   The emperor has the trumpets sound.
How fast his army covers the ground!
The men of Spain have turned their backs,
The French follow hard upon their tracks.
When the king sees the evening shadows,
He gets down from his horse, in a meadow,
Throws himself on the ground and prays
That God will stop the sun and cause
The fast approaching night to pause.
His ordinary angel comes
And rapidly gives his commands:
'The light will hold, Charles: so advance.
God knows you have lost the flower of France.
Take vengeance on the murderers.'
At this the emperor mounts his charger.

180   Then God performs a miracle
For Charlemagne; the sun stands still.
The pagans fly, the French follow
And catch up with them in a great hollow,
Val Ténébreux. They push them on
Their way to Saragossa town,
Killing them as they go. They cut
All the escape routes and pen them up
Where there is nowhere for them to go
Except the waters of the Ebro.
These are deep, dangerous and fast.
There is no boat or barge or raft.
The pagans call on Tervagant

To save them, but he won't or can't.
They jump in; those whose armour is heavy
Sink in the swirling water quickly:
The others float away downstream,
Some drink plenty, some haven't time.
All are in agony; all drown.
The French say: 'It's Roland sending you down!'

181   When Charles sees all the pagans dead,
Some killed, some drowned, and a few fled
And all his men loaded with booty,
The noble king dismounts. Once on foot
He falls on the ground to thank God.
When he gets up, the sun has gone.
The emperor says: 'We must camp here;
Our horses need rest, they are weary.
Too late for the Roncevalles now. Take off
Saddles and bridles and show them the grass;
Let them loose now in these meadows.'
The Franks reply: 'It shall be so.'

182   The emperor camps where he stands;
The French dismount in the empty land.
They take saddles and bridles off
And all the equipment dressed with gold,
Then they let the horses go,
There is nothing more they can do.
The weariest fall asleep on the ground.
No watch is kept and they sleep soundly.

183   The emperor lies in a meadow
Keeping his great spear by his pillow.
He did not want to disarm tonight.
He has on his hauberk, whose mail is white,
His helmet, still laced, with all its jewels,
Joyeuse buckled on, that has no equal
And thirty times a day changes colour.

90

We all know the lance the Roman soldier
Used at our Lord's crucifixion;
Charles has the point of it upon
The hilt of his sword, and set in gold.
It is for this reason, we are told
The sword was given the name, Joyeuse.
The French barons all know of this;
That is why they use the call
'Mountjoy!' and are invincible.

184   The night is clear and there is a moon,
Charles lies there but he is soon
Restless because of grief for Roland
And when he thinks of that stretch of land
By Roncevalles, with Oliver dead,
All the twelve peers, all dead and bloodied,
And all their men, he is in tears
And prays God keep their souls from fear.
The king is tired, his heart sore,
He has fallen asleep, he can do no more.
All over the meadow sleep the Franks,
Even the horses cannot stand,
Those who want grass lie down to eat.
Such wisdom can exhaustion teach.

185   Charles sleeps like a man in travail.
God has sent St Gabriel
To guard the emperor all night.
He does so. Charles sees a great light
And in a vision he is forewarned
Of a fierce battle: there are portents
Heavy with significance.
Charles looks up and all at once
Thunder and lightning, winds and hail,
Pelting rain, and then long tails
Of flame and flashes re-appear
And fall upon his army's spears.

The shafts of apple-wood and ash
Catch fire, and the shields catch
—Even the bosses of pure gold.
The shafts and even the spear-points fold,
Hauberks and steel helmets twist.
He sees his men in agonies.
Bears and leopards tear at them,
There are dragons, demons and serpents
And more than thirty thousand griffins
Are clawing at the Frenchmen's skin.
The French cry out: 'Help, Charlemagne!'
He feels pity for their pain
And wants to help, but cannot move.
A lion comes out of the wood
Attacking him with ferocity.
Both of them struggle breathlessly,
He does not know which is on top.
The emperor does not wake up.

186   After this vision, another one.
He is on a terrace in France,
In Aix, with a bear held by two chains.
Thirty more bears come from the Ardennes,
All of them have human speech.
They say: 'Give him to us!' and reach
Out. 'It's not right you should have him.
We have to help, we are his kin.'
From the king's palace a greyhound runs
And on the green grass, well beyond
The others, assails the largest bear.
Which will win? It is not clear.
God's angel brought this dream in the night
To Charles, who sleeps on till daylight.

187   King Marsilie, meanwhile, has fled
To Saragossa and dismounted
In the shade of an olive tree.

He has taken off his helmet and byrny
And lies on the ground miserably.
His right hand has entirely gone,
He is faint and suffering from loss of blood.
In front of him his wife Bramimond
Weeps and is anxious and despondent,
And twenty thousand men or more
Curse France and the emperor.
Then they make for Apollyon's crypt
And all the sanctuary is stripped.
Insultingly they shout: 'False god,
It is your fault our king has lost!
A poor reward for services!'
First his sceptre and crown are seized,
Then they hang him from the roof
But end by trampling him underfoot
And smashing him with sticks and clubs.
They take the jewels from Tervagant
And throw Mahomet into a ditch
To be destroyed by dogs and pigs.

188   Marsilie's recovered consciousness
And has himself carried, in distress,
To his vaulted chamber with painted walls.
Bramimond weeps for him and calls,
Tearing her hair, 'How wretched I am!'
Then, as clearly as she can:
'Saragossa, you are deprived
Of the king who gave you life!
Our gods have done a terrible wrong
In failing him when he was strong.
I will call the emir a coward outright
If he hesitates to fight
Against this people who are so proud,
So careless of their lives. No doubt
The emperor with the flowing beard
Is reckless and knows nothing of fear;

He will not run away from a battle!
Ah, if only he could be killed!'

189 The emperor has now maintained
His forces for seven years in Spain;
He has taken castles and many cities.
King Marsilie has resisted
And he has sent letters with great seals on
To Baligant in Babylon
—The emir who has lived longer than
Virgil or Homer or any man:
He was to come to Saragossa
Or the king would see that his idols suffered
And he would worship them no more
But would accept the Christian law
And do a deal with Charlemagne.
The emir is far off, the time
Goes on, he does not come. He sends
His messengers to forty lands,
Telling his people to prepare
Great ships and barges everywhere.
This navy he collects in port
By Alexandria, ready to depart.
The first day of summer, proudly
The whole armada puts to sea.

190 They have great armies, this hostile race.
They sail and row at a great pace.
On topmasts and on prows there rise
All manner of brilliants and of lights
Which throw their radiance so far
The sea is brighter than with stars,
And as they come to the coast of Spain
The whole land is lit up as plain
As if it were daylight. Then quickly
The news is brought to Marsilie.

191 The pagan people push on faster,
Come from the sea into fresh water;
They pass Marbrise and pass Marbrose;
Soon they are heading up the Ebro.
Their lanterns give light all the way
And they are in Saragossa next day.

192 The sun shines and the day is clear.
The emir has now gone ashore.
Espaneliz walks at his right hand;
Seventeen kings follow him and
Innumerable dukes and counts.
There is a laurel, on level ground,
It stands in the middle of the stretch,
And there a white carpet has been set
On the green grass, on that a throne
Of ivory and there sits Baligant.
The others round him remain standing
And he speaks to them like a king:
'Listen, you who would earn my thanks.
Charles, the emperor of the Franks
Is to eat no crumb unless I say.
He has made war on me in Spain;
Now I will look for him in France,
Not stopping for any chance
Till I have him alive or dead.'
He slapped his knee with his glove as he said this.

193 He has spoken. He has given his word
That, for all the gold in the world
He will not be stopped from going to Aix
To reckon with Charles in his own place.
His men praise him and give advice.
Then he summons two of his knights,
Clarifan and Clariën:
'You are the sons of Maltraïen
Who once was my ambassador.

Go to Saragossa and there
Tell Marsilie, as from me,
I have come to help him with my army
Against the French, as they will discover.
When you have said that, give him this glove
And see that he puts it on his right hand.
Take for him too this golden staff
And tell him to come here and do homage.
I will go fighting Charles in France.
If he doesn't grovel and call for mercy
And deny the laws of Christianity
I will have the crown off of his head.'
The pagans answer: 'Sir, well said.'

194   Baligant says: 'Now ride off.
One take the glove, the other the staff!'
And they reply: 'Sir, we will go.'
They ride till they reach Saragossa.
They pass ten gates and four bridges
And the streets full of citizens.
When they get to the top of the town
Where the palace is, they hear a sound:
The pagans weep and mourn; their gods,
Every one of them, are lost:
Tervagant, Apollo, Mahomet,
Nothing of any of them is left.
'What will happen to us?' they ask,
'What help shall we have in any task?
Now we are in utter confusion;
King Marsilie's days are done,
Roland cut off his right hand;
Jurfaleu the Fair is dead and
All Spain is at their mercy now!'
The messengers appear, and dismount.

195   Under the olive-tree they leave
Their horses, and the reins are seized

By Saracens. The messengers,
Each holding the other's cloak with his fingers,
Climb to the highest part of the palace.
Into the vaulted chamber they pass
With loving greeting, unlucky words:
'May Mahomet, whom all of us serve,
Save the king and keep the queen!'
Bramimond says: 'Where has he been?
Doesn't he know we have been betrayed
By our gods, and what trick they have played
At Roncevalles, where they let our men
Be killed and did not defend
My lord? They failed him in the battle and
Permitted the loss of his right hand;
The mighty Roland cut it off;
Charles will have all Spain from us!
What will happen to me, I am unhappy!
Will no man kill me out of mercy?'

196 Says Clariën: 'You talk on and on.
We are the messengers of Baligant.
He will look after Marsilie
And send him, as a guarantee,
His staff and glove. Upon the Ebro
We have four thousand vessels and more,
Barges, lighters, rapid galleys,
So many, I cannot say how many.
The emir is a powerful man
And is going to look for Charles in France;
He will get him, alive or dead.'
'He is looking too far!' Bramimond says.
'You'll find the Franks are closer than that;
They've already been seven years in this land.
The emperor knows how to fight
And he would die rather than retreat.
Does he fear a king? Does he fear a child!
Charles does not fear any man alive.'

197   'Enough of that!' says Marsilie.
       Then to the messengers: 'Speak to me!
       You see a man whose death is near.
       I have no son, daughter, nor any heir.
       I had a son, killed yesterday.
       Go to your lord and mine and say
       He should come here, Spain is his by right,
       I will yield it to him as soon as he likes.
       Then let him defend it against the French!
       If he listens to me, I shall be revenged
       And he will have Charles within a month.
       Take the keys of Saragossa town
       And tell him not to go away.'
       They reply: 'We will do as you say.'

198   Marsilie says: 'The emperor
       Has killed my men and raged over
       My land, destroying my cities.
       I'll tell you how far away he is:
       Last night he slept beside the Ebro,
       Seven leagues from here, let the emir know.
       Tell him, now is the time for battle.'
       He gives them the keys of Saragossa.
       The messengers, both of them, bow,
       Take their leave and off they go.

199   The messengers mount and quickly
       They are riding out of the city,
       Excitedly, back to the emir.
       They give the keys as soon as they're there.
       Baligant says: 'What did you find out?
       Where's Marsilie? Did you come without
       Him in spite of what I said?'
       Says Clariën: 'He is half-dead.
       The emperor was in the pass
       Yesterday, on the way to France.
       He left a noble rear-guard. Roland,

Who is his nephew, in command,
With Oliver and all twelve peers
And twenty thousand armed French soldiers.
King Marsilie fought with them.
He and Roland met and then
Roland struck him with Durandal,
At which he saw his right hand fall.
His son was killed, his dearest son
And all the accompanying barons.
Marsilie fled, he could do no other,
With the emperor following close after.
That is what the king wants help against.
He gives up all his rights in Spain.'
When Baligant reflects on this
He is grieved to the point of madness.

200 'Emir,' says Clarien, 'Yesterday
Was a battle in Roncevalles, they say.
Roland was killed, and Oliver
And all the twelve peers Charles held dear.
Twenty thousand French were killed.
Marsilie lost his right hand, he will
Tell how the emperor followed his flight
And did not leave him a single knight;
All were killed or drowned in the Ebro.
The emperor camped on its banks:
So close to us are the Franks.
You can still stop them going home.'
Baligant jumped from his throne;
His look is proud and he is happy.
He calls out: 'Come on my lords, hurry!
Disembark, get into the saddle, and go!
If Charlemagne does not withdraw
Marsilie will be soon avenged:
In place of his hand we'll have Charles's head.'

201   The pagans from Arabia
Have disembarked, and without delay
Have mounted horses or mounted mules,
And ridden off. What else should they do?
The emir who ordered all this movement
Calls Gemalfin, a trusted man:
'I put you in command of my armies.'
Then he mounts on his chestnut charger
And, taking with him four of his dukes,
Rides to Saragossa and at the foot
Of a marble staircase he dismounts,
His stirrup held by four of the counts.
He is going up the palace stairs
When, running, Bramimond appears;
She says to him: 'Things have gone badly.
I have lost my lord, and shamefully!'
She falls at his feet, he raises her
And together they go to the chamber.

202   When king Marsilie sees Baligant
He tells two of his Saracens
To lift him so that he sits up.
In his left hand he takes a glove
And says to the emir: 'Sir, take this,
And all my lands, with Saragossa,
I cannot keep them now with honour.
I have lost myself and my people.'
The emir answers: 'I am grieved.
I cannot stay, I have seen enough
And none the less I take your glove.'
With that he turns weeping away
Then, down the palace steps again.
He mounts his horse, applies his spurs
And rides till he is riding first.
At every moment he repeats:
'Come on, they are in retreat!'

203   That morning, when the dawn first showed
        The emperor Charlemagne awoke.
        Saint Gabriel, whom God sent to his side,
        Raises his hand and makes his sign.
        The king then lays aside his arms;
        All do the same throughout the army.
        Then they mount and they ride fast
        By long and broad roads to the pass.
        They are going to view the murderous
        Roncevalles, where the battle was.

204   Charles has reached the Roncevalles
        And weeps to see what happened to all
        His men there. Then he says to the French:
        'My lords, if you please ride gently.
        It must be I who have the first view
        For I want to find Roland, my nephew.
        In Aix once, at a solemn feast
        When all my knights were making their boast
        Of what battles they would fight,
        I heard Roland claim as a right
        That he would not die in a foreign land
        Unless he were ahead of all his men
        With his face turned towards the enemy:
        His death would be a victory.'
        A stone's throw from the rest
        The emperor climbs up to a crest.

205   The emperor, looking for his nephew,
        Finds many flowering plants bedewed
        With many French barons' blood:
        No wonder his tears came in a flood!
        So under two trees he stops
        Where Roland struck the marble blocks.
        He recognises whose strokes those are
        And his nephew lies on the green grass there.
        No wonder his grief is beyond solace;

He dismounts and runs where the body is.
With both his hands he lifts it up
Then falls faint on it, so great his love.

206   The emperor recovers consciousness:
Then he sees the good duke Naimès,
Count Acelin, Geoffrey of Anjou
And his brother Henry too.
They prop him against a tree.
He looks again. What does he see?
His nephew Roland lying there.
Very gently, and full of care,
He takes leave of him: 'My friend
Roland,' he says, 'this is the end.
God have mercy on you. No man
Fought such great battles and won.
My honour enters its decline.'
Charles swoons a second time.

207   Charles is conscious again, and finds
Four of his barons at his sides
Holding his hands. He looks down
And sees his nephew on the ground:
A handsome body, without colour,
Eyes turned up and full of shadow.
In faith and love Charles laments:
'God set your soul in flowers, my friend
Roland, in Paradise, in glory!
You were sent to Spain for a sad story!
No day but I shall suffer for it.
For strength and ardour now unfit,
Who shall sustain my honour, or how?
I have no friend on earth, although
Kinsmen are there, but who so daring?'
With both hands he pulls out his hair.
A hundred thousand French are grieved;
There is not one of them but weeps.

208   'Roland, I shall go back to France
And when in Laon I rest my lance
My vassals will come flocking in
From many kingdoms, all asking:
"Where is the count who was your captain?"
I shall say, he was lost in Spain.
I shall be king, but in sorrow;
Weeping today, weeping tomorrow.

209   'Roland, courageous, lovely youth,
How shall I tell my vassals the truth
When I am in my chapel in Aix?
"What news?" they will ask, and I shall say:
"Bad news, extraordinary, but bad;
My nephew, the great conqueror, is dead."
And then the Saxons will rebel,
Hungarians and Bulgars as well,
Malcontents, Romans, Palernians,
Africans and Califernians.
There will be trouble again
And who will lead my forces then
When he is not there to command?
France is a desolated land
And I no longer want to live!'
He tears his white beard and is
In such distraction a hundred thousand
French fall senseless on the ground.

210   'Roland, God grant you all his mercies!
May your soul rest in Paradise!
The man who killed you ruined France.
I would not live in such mischance,
With all my household dead for me.
May God, the son of Saint Mary,
Allow my soul to leave this carcass
Before I reach the border pass,
And find its place among the souls

And burial among them for my corpse!'
He weeps and tugs at his white beard
And Naimès says: 'The emperor!'

211   'Sir,' says Geoffrey of Anjou,
'Do not let this grief master you!
Order a search over the field
For all our men the Spanish killed.
Have them put in a common pit.'
The king said: 'Sound your horn! See to it!'

212   Geoffrey of Anjou sounds his horn.
As Charles has ordered, the French dismount.
They seek out all their friends who have died
And lay them in the pit side by side.
There are many bishops and abbots there,
Monks, canons, tonsured priests. They are
Soon busy with the absolution
Of the bodies, and benediction.
They light the myrrh and each body
Collected is censed vigorously;
Then they are buried with great honour
And left, for what can men do more?

213   For Roland, Turpin and Oliver
The emperor has a special care.
The bodies are opened before his eyes
And the hearts wrapped in silken covers.
Each is put in a marble coffin.
Then the three lords' bodies are sewn in
The hides of deer, when they have been
Washed with spices and with wine.
The king gives orders then to Tibbald,
Geboin, Milon and Oton for all
To be taken back on three waggons
With silks of Galaza spread on them.

214 He would go with them, the emperor
But then the pagan vanguard appears.
From the first troop, two messengers
Announce a battle, as from the emir:
'Proud king, you will not so easily
Get away, for there you may see
Baligant riding after you.
His Arabian armies are on the move;
He will test your courage today, and here.'
Charles's hand goes to his beard,
He thinks of all that he has lost.
Then proudly he looks at his own host
And calls out at the top of his voice:
'Now, French barons, to arms and to horse!'

215 The emperor is the first to be ready.
Quickly he puts on his byrny,
Laces his helmet, buckles his sword,
Joyeuse, bright as ever before;
Hangs round his neck his Biterne shield,
Waves his spear towards the field
Then he mounts Tencendur, his horse
—Which he took below Marsonne, at the ford
When he threw Malpalin dead from the saddle.
He applies his spurs and rides to battle,
First galloping in front of his men
Calling on God and the apostle of Rome.

216 The French have dismounted everywhere;
Ten thousand of them are arming there.
They are well equipped, their horses are fast,
They are highly trained and they are well placed.
If battle comes they will know what to do.
Over their helmets to and fro
Their banners swing. Charles looks at his men
And says to the Provençal Jozeran,
Duke Naimès and Antelme de Mayence:

'Those are the vassals to justify France!
With such men anything can be done.
If the Arabs are not afraid to come
They will pay dear for Roland's death.'
Duke Naimès says: 'For God and the faith!'

217   Charles calls Rabel and Guinemant:
The king says: 'This is my command:
You replace Roland and Oliver,
One take the sword, the horn the other,
And ride ahead, the two of you
With fifteen thousand French, the youth
From among my best fighting men.
After that the like again,
Geboin and Lodranz at their head.'
Duke Naimès and Jorzeran ordered
These arrangements. All is done
To prepare for the great battle to come.

218   The first two columns are all French.
After them and next in strength
The vassals from Bavaria,
Perhaps twenty thousand of them there;
They are men who will not give way.
Charles loves them better than any
Except the French, who conquered them
And won the kingdoms for Charlemagne.
They are a proud company
Which Ogier of Denmark will lead.

219   After these columns Naimès forms
Another one, it is the fourth,
Of barons on whom Charles can rely.
These are Germans from Germany:
Twenty thousand, so it is said.
They are well horsed, and fitted
With all they need in the way of arms.

They would sooner die than show alarm.
Hermann will lead them, the duke of Thrace
Who looks his enemies in the face.

220   Duke Naimès and count Jozeran
Have made up a fifth group, the Normans,
Twenty thousand, the French say;
Well armed, with fast horses, they
Would rather die than surrender.
Nowhere are there better fighters.
Richard the Old will lead them here.
He is a good man with a spear.

221   The sixth group is made up of Bretons,
There are thirty thousand of them.
They look like proper warriors,
With painted spears and flying banners.
The name of their lord is Eudon.
He tells count Nevelon,
Tibbald of Reims, Oton the marquess
To command his men and the honour is theirs.

222   The emperor has six columns,
Now there are to be seven of them:
Poitevins and the Auvergne barons,
There might be forty thousand men.
There are good horses and arms for all,
They form in a valley, under a hill.
Charles blesses them with his right hand.
Godselm and Jozeran are in command.

223   Naimès draws up the eighth column
Of Flemings and of Frisian barons.
There are forty thousand more,
Never known to give up before.
The king says: 'They will serve again.'
Who is to command these men?

Rembalt and Hamon the Galician
Are jointly given this position.

224   Naimès and Jozeran together
Form a ninth column of riders,
Men from Lorraine and Burgundy,
Fifty thousand, there are reckoned to be,
In byrnies, with helmets laced.
They have short strong spears which, well placed,
Will give the Arabs trouble enough
If they don't call the battle off;
These men will hit them hard, set on
By Thierry, he is duke of Argonne.

225   The tenth group are all French barons,
A hundred thousand of our best captains,
Men of proud looks and appearance
With flowing hair and long white beards.
They wear hauberks or double byrnies,
French or Spanish swords; each in turn is
Displaying his colours on his shield.
They are keen to be in the field.
They shout 'Mountjoy!' Charles is with them,
Geoffrey of Anjou bears the oriflamme
—Once at St Peter's, the Roman flag
But now called Mountjoy; they changed it to that

226   The emperor gets down from his horse
And lies face down in the green grass.
Turning his face towards the east
He calls on God: his words are these:
'True Father, so defend me this day
As you did Jonah, when he lay
Deep in the belly of the whale;
And, as before you did not fail
The king of Nineveh, or as when
Daniel was in the lions' den

And you saved him from that strange torture;
As you saved the three children in the fire,
So your love be with me today!
Grant, of your mercy, that I may
Have vengeance for my nephew Roland!'
When he has prayed and is once more standing
He makes the sign of the cross on his head.
The king mounts, while the stirrup is held
By Naimès and by Jozeran;
He takes his short and sharp lance,
A noble figure, certainly,
Looking round contentedly.
He rides like an accomplished horseman.
Trumpets sound in the rear and van;
Above them all sounds Roland's horn
And the French weep for him that morning.

227   Nobly the emperor rides
In his byrny, with his beard outside.
For love of him the others put
Their beards out and by that the troop,
His hundred thousand French, will know
Whom to trust and whom to follow.
They pass the peaks and towering rocks,
The deep valleys, the narrow tracks,
Passes and wild land, back to Spain.
They have marched down into the plain
And there it is they take their stand.
The scouts have come back to Baligant.
A Syrian has given him this warning:
'We have seen Charles, the haughty king.
His men are proud, they will not fail him.
Arm now, you will have battle today!'
Baligant says: 'I would have it so.
Trumpets! Let my pagans know!'

228 All through the army sound the drums,
Then the bugles and trumpets come in:
The pagans all dismount to arm.
The emir himself is not tardy,
He puts on his byrny of burnished mail,
Laces his helmet, bright with jewels,
Then buckles his sword at his left side.
What name should he give it, in his pride,
Except the name Charles gave his sword?
'Précieuse' is what it is called
And that serves too as his battle-cry;
He calls it now and his men reply.
Then he hangs his great shield round his neck,
The boss is golden, crystal the edge,
The strap is silk with circles on it.
He takes his spear, which he calls Maltet,
The handle-end is like a club,
The metal part enough for a mule-load.
Baligant mounts upon his charge,
Marcules holding the stirrup. He is large,
The emir, and tremendous astride;
He has broad ribs and slender sides;
He has a deep, well-muscled chest,
Big shoulders, a fine complexion
And wears on his face a proud expression,
His white curled hair is like flowers in summer!
No doubt that he will face all comers!
What he would be as a Christian, God knows!
He spurs his horse till the blood flows.
He canters around and jumps a ditch
Fifty feet wide, men measured it.
The pagans cry: 'What a man for the marches!
There isn't a single Frenchman could touch him!
To encounter him means death or defeat:
Charles is a fool not to retreat.'

229 The emir is like a proper baron,
His beard is so white and flowing,
He is so learned in his law
And in battle he is best of all.
His son Malprimis has great valour,
He is tall and strong like his ancestors.
He says to his father: 'Sir, we must
Hurry or else Charles will escape us!'
Baligant says: 'No, he's no coward,
There are endless stories of his prowess;
But now he is without his nephew
Roland, he'll find his men too few.'

230 'Malprimis, my fine son,' Baligant
Answers him, 'They have killed Roland
And Oliver, his brave companion
And the twelve peers, Charles's best men,
And twenty thousand French as well.
The rest of them are negligible.
The emperor's coming back, I know,
The Syrian has told me so,
Ten columns of them, maybe more.
They have a good man sounding that horn
And his companion's trumpet answers:
Those are the two who lead the advance;
They ride ahead, in company
With fifteen thousand of the French gentry,
Bachelors Charles calls his children.
Then follows another column of them.
They will fight, and proudly too.'
Malprimis says: 'May I strike the first blow?'

231 'Malprimis, son,' Baligant says,
'Yes, I will grant your request;
You shall have first go at the French.
Take with you Torleu, a good friend
And who is king of Persia,

And another king from Leuticia.
If you can tame the enemy's pride
I will give you all that side
Of my land from Cheriant to Val Marchis.'
He replies: 'Sir, if you please!'
He advances and receives the gift;
It is where the king Flori lived
At that time: he was never to see it
Or take possession of his fief.

232   The emir rides among his troops,
His son follows, a well-made youth.
King Torleu and king Dapamort
Make thirty columns, of every sort
Of people in that immense host.
What a company he can boast!
The smallest column has fifty thousand
Men. The first comes from the land
Of Butenrot, the second set
Are all Myconians, with broad heads,
They have bristles down their spines
As if they were not men but swine;
The third from Nublès and from Blos
The fourth from Braunscheig and the Slav coast,
The fifth are Sorbians, from Sorb,
The sixth Armenians and Moors,
The seventh are men from Jericho,
The eighth Negroes, the ninth from Gros,
The tenth from the fort at Balida,
Not friends with anyone, they say.
The emir swears as pagans will
By Mahomet and his miracles:
'Charles of France is mad to ride
This way and, unless he retires,
He will have battle, but will lie down
Tonight without his golden crown.'

233 They form another ten columns,
The first of Canaanites, and ugly,
From Val Fuiten, the crooked way;
Next Turks, then Persians, so they say;
The fourth from Petchenek and Pers,
The fifth from Solteras and Avers,
The sixth from Ormaleus and Eugiel,
The seventh, the tribe of Samuel,
The eighth from Bruise, the ninth Clavers,
The tenth from Occian, the desert;
A people who do not serve God,
A criminal and murderous lot,
Their skins are harder than any iron,
They put no other armour on,
Neither helmet nor hauberk, they are
Difficult men to meet in war.

234 The emir adds ten columns to those:
The first, of giants from Malprose,
The second Huns, the third Hungarians,
The fourth from the Baghdad area,
The fifth from the Val Peneuse,
The sixth of men from Maruse,
The seventh from Leus and Astrimoines,
The eighth from Argoilles, the ninth from Clarbonne,
The tenth bearded men from Fronde,
A race of people hostile to God.
So they were, the thirty columns
Spoken of in the *Gesta Francorum*.
Through these great armies trumpets sound:
The pagans ride to the battle ground.

235 The emir is a powerful man.
In front of him they carry his dragon,
Tervagant's standard and Mahomet's
And Apollyon's image. Ten Canaanites
Escort him, riding round about:

Altogether they call out:
'Pray to our gods and serve them humbly,
All who hope for any safety!'
The pagans bow their heads, and their helmets
Touch the ground, gleaming. The French
Mutter: 'You devils must die!
May it go ill with you today!'
Then: 'God our God, protect Charlemagne
In this battle we fight in his name!'

236   The emir is wily and discerning;
He calls his sons and the two kings.
'Lord barons, you will ride ahead
And command all my columns,' he says,
'But I will keep three of the best:
One of Turks, the Ormaleans next
And third, the giants of Malprose.
I shall take the men of Occian, those
Will attack Charles and the French.
If the emperor ventures his strength
With me, I'll have his head off his shoulders.
He will never grow any older.'

237   Nothing between the armies now,
Not a hill or valley or even a row
Of bushes. No concealment there:
Across the empty plain they stare.
Baligant says: 'Now all who hate
Christianity, make haste!
Ride into battle now.' Amborres
From Aleppo it is who carries
The standard. All the pagans shout
'Précieuse!' The French call loudly:
'May this day end badly for you!'
And cries of 'Mountjoy!' are renewed.
Trumpets sound for the emperor
And above them all, the great horn.

The pagans say: 'These troops of Charles's
Will make a fight of it, and hard.'

238   Wide the plain and broad the view:
Helmets shine with gold and jewels,
Shields shine, and burnished mail,
The spears, the pennons with long tails.
The trumpets call, their voices clear,
The horn sounds the following of the deer.
The emir summons Canabeu
Who is the king of Floridee,
Whose land runs to the Cloven Valley.
He points to Charles's arrayed army:
'There is the boasted power of France!
The emperor has taken his stand
At the rear with those bearded men.
They have put their beards out over their chests,
White as snow fallen on ice!
They will strike with swords and lances;
The battle will be hard and tough
As any ever known to us.'
Baligant and his escort ride
A stone's-throw in front of the pagan side
For all to hear what he has to say:
'Come on, I will lead the way!'
He brandishes his lance and turns
The point towards Charles, in scorn.

239   Charlemagne sees the emir's dragon,
Banner and standard, and all the men
The Arabs have assembled there;
So many they are everywhere
Except the ground the emperor holds.
The king of France cries out boldly:
'French barons, you are good vassals!
The victors in how many fields!
There are the pagans: murderers, cowards!

If they are numerous, be it so!
Let those who are not with me go!'
He spurs his great horse, Tencendur
Who makes four capers in the air.
The French say: 'Our king will not fail,
Nor we him; we shall not turn tail!'

240   The day is clear, the sun brilliant,
The armies are magnificent.
The first ranks now face each other,
Rabel and Guinemant together
Give their swift horses their heads.
They touch them with their spurs. The French
Let themselves go to the attack,
Spears ready, shields about their necks.

241   Count Rabel's a courageous rider,
His gold spurs touch his horse's sides,
He charges Torleu, the Persian king,
Shield and byrny cannot withstand him,
His spear has gone through the king's guts
And thrown him off into the scrub.
The French say: 'God keep us in his sight!
We'll not fail; Charles is in the right.'

242   Guinemant attacks a Lycian king
And smashes his flowered shield, tearing
After that, right through his byrny
And drives his pennon through his body
So, dead as a doornail, down he goes.
The French shout at the marvellous blow:
'Fight on, this is no time for doubt;
Charles is right and we are sent
To carry out God's true judgement.'

243   Malprimis, mounted on a white horse,
Throws himself against the French force;

He strikes blows on all sides and leaves
Dead piled upon dead in heaps.
Baligant cries before them all:
'My barons, you have fed in my hall:
Now see my son, seeking the French
King and challenging his strength.
There is no better vassal here.
Help him now with your sharp spears!'
At these words the pagans advance
Against the fighting men of France;
No battle was ever so terrifying
Either before or since that time.

244   There are great armies, the troops are brave
And all the columns are engaged.
The pagans fight miraculously.
There are broken spears, God! how many?
Shields smashed and armour spoiled.
The grass is strewn with pieces, the soil
Churned up where the green grass was
. . . . .
The emir calls up his men:
'Strike at them now, strike at the Christians!'
It is a hard battle, this one.
Never was there such another;
Night will fall before it is over.

245   The emir calls his people: 'Strike,
Pagans: you are here to fight!
You shall have women, well-born, beautiful
With lands and honours enough for all.'
The pagans answer: 'We will not stint.'
They use their spears till they fall in splinters;
More than a hundred thousand swords
Are drawn, and with them they press forward.
Anyone who saw that horrible
Sword-play has indeed seen battle.

246   The emperor sppeals to the French:
      'My lords, I love you, trust your strength.
      So many battles you have fought
      For me, so many kingdoms bought
      With blood, and sent their kings packing!
      Well I know what I owe you—everything,
      My body, lands, possessions, all.
      Avenge those who in Roncevalles
      Last night were killed, your sons, your brothers,
      Your heirs. You know where justice lies,
      Not with the pagans!' 'Sir, we are apprised!'
      Answer the Franks, and twenty thousand then
      Promise that they will always be his men,
      Come what may come, anguish or death,
      Their lances serve him till their last breath.
      Instantly they draw their swords;
      Bitterly the battle goes forward.

247   Malprimis rides through the battlefield
      And many of the French are felled.
      Duke Naimès looks proudly at the prince
      And valiantly goes to attack him.
      He breaks the shield's upper edge,
      Tears open the hauberk and wedges
      His yellow pennon in the prince's body
      And leaves him dead—among so many!

248   King Canabeu, the emir's brother
      Spurs his horse when he sees trouble;
      He draws his sword with the crystal hilt
      And strikes duke Naimès on the helmet.
      He splits it cleanly in two pieces
      And with his sword cuts five of the laces.
      The hood of mail gives no protection,
      He slices to the flesh, one section
      Of the mail is cut away.
      The duke is stunned, the blow is so heavy;

He would have fallen then and there
Had not God rescued him. His charger
Stood, he put his arms around his neck.
If the pagan had at once come back
The noble vassal would have died.
But Charles of France, his king, arrived.

249   Duke Naimès is in great distress.
The pagan again begins to press
Upon his enemy. Charles the king
Says: 'You have done a fatal thing!'
He breaks, taking duke Naimès' part,
The pagan's shield upon his heart;
Then slashing the hauberk neck he lightly
Leaves him dead and his saddle empty.

250   Charlemagne is filled with grief
When he sees Naimès' wounds are deep
And his blood flowing on the green grass.
The emperor says to him: 'Naimès!
Good sir, now ride along with me!
The rascal who had you in difficulty
Lies dead with my spear through his neck.'
The duke replies: 'Sir, you know best.
If I live, you will not regret it.'
Then side by side they go, in friendship;
With them go twenty thousand French,
Keeping the enemy at sword's length.

251   The emir rides over the plain
To attack the count Guinemant.
He breaks his white shield on his heart
And tears off pieces of his hauberk
Severing his left ribs from his right,
And throwing him dead from his horse. He strikes
Dead at once Geboin and Lorant
And Richard the Old, who leads the Normans.

The pagans cry: 'Précieuse is valiant!
Fight on, barons, we have a champion!'

252 Could you have seen all those Arabians,
Men of Occiant, Macedonians!
How well they handle their spears! How well
The Frenchmen stand their ground. There fall
Many on one side and the other:
Evening, and there is still battle.
How many barons does France lose?
There will be more before the close.

253 French and Arabs both fight well.
Everywhere, splintered lances fall.
You should have seen the broken shields
And heard the battered hauberks creak,
Shields squeal upon the helmets
And men falling as they are hit,
Bellowing and dying on the ground:
You would not forget such sights and sounds!
It is a hard battle for some:
The emir calls upon Apollyon,
Tervagant and Mahomet, all three:
'I have served you, lord gods, and see!
I will make your images in gold!'
. . . . .
Gemalfin, the trusted, reports to him,
Bringing him the worst of news:
'Baligant, sire, here is sorrow for you!
You have lost Malprimis, your son
And Canbeu, your brother, has gone;
Two Frenchmen had this success.
The emperor's one of them, I guess:
A big man, he looked a great lord,
With a beard as white as April flowers.'
The emir bows his helmet and
His face is turned towards the ground;

He thinks he will die, he is so grieved.
He calls Jongleu, from overseas.

254   The emir says: 'Come here, Jongleu,
I have no wiser man than you;
I have always followed your advice.
Who do you think will win this fight?
Will it be the Arabians or the Franks?'
He replied: 'You are a dead man,
Baligant; your gods will do nothing
To help you against Charles the king;
Never were men so warlike as his.
But call your barons while there is
Yet time, Turks, men of Occiant,
Come what may, the Arabs and the Giants!'

255   He has put his beard outside, the emir,
It is white as hawthorn flower;
He is not looking for concealment,
Happen what will. He puts his trumpet
To his lips and sounds it clearly.
All over the field the pagans hear
And his companions rally to him.
The men of Occiant bay and whinny,
Those from Arguille yap like dogs.
They challenge the French, though it is folly.
They cut their way through the thick of them
And leave dead seven thousand men.

256   Count Ogier was never a coward,
Better man never put on armour.
When he sees the break in the French columns
He calls Thierry, the duke of Argonne,
Geoffrey of Anjou and Jozeran
And speaks proudly as the king's man:
'See how the pagans are striking down
Your men; may you not wear the crown

Unless you avenge this dishonour!'
Nobody speaks another word;
Spurring their horses on, they charge
And bear down on the enemy hard.

257 Charlemagne's blows are marvellous;
Duke Naimès and Ogier do no less
Well, nor does Geoffrey of Anjou
Who fights and bears the standard too.
Ogier the Dane above all:
He spurs his horse to a gallop and falls
Upon the man who carries the dragon,
So that Amboire crashes down,
With him the dragon and the king's standard.
Baligant sees his banner foundered
And Mahomet's emblem in the dust:
Then the emir begins to distrust
His gods and sees that Charles is right.
The pagan Arabs think of flight.
The emperor calls to the French:
'For God's sake, barons, show your strength!'
The French reply: 'No need to ask;
Our honour binds us to this task.'

258 The day is passing, evening draws
On; and now all use their swords,
Franks and pagans, and they are
Brave men on both sides in this war.
Neither forgets its battle-cry:
The emir's 'Précieuse!' on one side
And Charles's 'Mountjoy!' on the other
And so the two kings come together,
Recognising each other's voices;
They fight in the middle of the field,
Striking each other's studded shields
Till both break under the broad bosses;
They rip each other's hauberks, their horses'

Girths are broken and down go
Both kings from their saddles and so
Have to scramble to their feet;
They draw their swords, and again meet.
Both will fight while they have breath;
The battle can end only with a death.

259   Charles of sweet France is valiant, the emir
Is not a coward or a doubter.
They brandish naked swords, each gives
Great blows upon the other's shield which
Cut the leather and double boards;
The nails fly out, the bosses fall;
Unprotected except for their byrnies
They fight on; sparks as from a furnace
Rise from their helmets; and until
One admits he is wrong, they will.

260   The emir says: 'Now, Charles, reflect
On the ill you have done to me, and repent!
You have killed my son, as well I know
And your claim to my country is hollow.
You should become my vassal, ready
To do me service faithfully
Both here and in the east.' Charles says:
'It would bring shame to all of us.
Peace and love are not for pagans.
Receive God's law, the law of Christians
And I will begin to love you at once.
Serve and trust God's omnipotence.'
Baligant says: 'That is evil talk.'
They took their swords again, and fought.

261   The emir with all his might and main
Strikes at the head of Charlemagne.
The burnished helmet breaks and splits;
The sword slices the scalp and it

Takes a handsbreadth of the flesh;
The bone shows, but Charles is not vanquished.
He totters, surely he must fall?
But no! for God wills his survival.
St Gabriel comes back to him
And says: 'Why hesitate, great king?'

262   Charles hears the angel's holy voice;
He has no fear, he has no choice;
Quickly he comes out of his trance
And once more wields the sword of France
Breaking the emir's helmet, the jewels
Glitter, but he has smashed the skull,
Cleaving the face to the white beard:
There is no recovery for the emir.
The emperor shouts 'Mountjoy!' to rally
Around him all his company.
Naimès the duke comes, he has found
Tencendur, and the king remounts.
The pagans fly, God wills it so.
The French face a defeated foe.

263   The pagans flee, by the will of God,
The Franks and the emperor in pursuit.
The king says: 'Lords, avenge your grief
And give your hearts and minds relief;
This morning I have seen your tears.'
And the Franks answer: 'Have no fear!'
They lay about them, one and all;
Few they encounter do not fall.

264   The heat is great, the dust rises,
The pagans flee and fall under the eyes
Of the French, right into the town
Of Saragossa where, high in her tower
Bramimond climbs with all her crowd
Of clergy, the men of the false law,

Untonsured, with no orders at all.
Seeing the Arabs in disarray
She cries: 'Mahomet, give us aid!
Good king, our men are conquered now,
The emir shamefully brought us low!'
Marsilie hears and turns his face
Away, he weeps for his disgrace;
So dies of grief, in all his sins,
And yields his soul to living demons.

265   They are dead, the pagans, most of them
And Charles has won the battle. His men
Have battered down the massive gates:
Saragossa is left to its fate.
He knows it will not be defended,
He takes possession, the day has ended,
The victorious army settles down,
The king with the white beard is proud.
And Bramimond has given up
The towers to his guardianship,
The ten big ones, the fifty small.
Who trusts God may accomplish all.

266   The day has passed and it is night,
The moon is clear and there is starlight.
Saragossa has been taken.
A thousand Frenchmen search the place,
Its synagogues and mosques, and smash
With iron sledge-hammers and axes
The images and all the idols
Till nothing is left of all their lies.
The king believes in the God he serves.
The bishops speak their holy words
Over the water, and they lead
The pagans to the baptistry:
Any who opposes Charles's will
Is hung or burnt or otherwise killed.

A hundred thousand are baptised
True Christians, but the queen not at this time.
She is to go to France as a captive,
The king would have her converted by love.

267   The night goes. In the morning hours
Charles posts men on all the towers;
He leaves four thousand well-trained men
To keep the town in the emperor's name.
The king mounts, his barons with him,
And Bramimond, whom he takes to her prison
But he does not wish her any harm.
They are in high spirits as they return.
They storm Narbonne with energy
And reach Bordeaux; in that famous city
Charles puts the horn upon the altar
Of Saint Séverin, filled with gold:
There pilgrims can see it still.
He crosses the Gironde with oars and sail;
He conducts his nephew's body to Blaye,
His companion Oliver's, and the sage
And gallant Turpin's, the archbishop.
In marble coffins they are put
At Saint Romain: and there they lie,
Commended to the Trinity.
Over hills and valleys Charles rides away
Not stopping till he reaches Aix.
He rides up to the palace steps.
When he is inside, he sends
His messengers to summon his judges,
Bavarians, Saxons, Lorrains, Frisians;
He summons Germans and Burgundians.
Poitevins, Normans and Bretons
And the French who are the wisest men:
Then begins the trial of Ganelon.

268   The emperor is back from Spain
In the best castle in France, at Aix;
He climbs to his palace; in the hall
Aude approaches, the loveliest of all
The ladies there. She asks him: 'Where
Is Roland, the captain? Did he not swear
That he would take me as his wife?'
Great tears appear in Charles's eyes,
He tugs his white beard and says:
'Sister, it is a dead man you ask
For, I will give you the best I can:
Louis, there is no better man;
He is my son and will keep the marches.'
Aude replies: 'You break my heart.
Please God, his saints and angels, I
Will not live since Roland has died.'
She loses her colour and falls down
Before the feet of Charlemagne,
Dead in an instant. God have mercy
On her soul! The French weep for pity.

269   The lovely Aude has finished her days.
The king thinks she is in a faint.
The emperor weeps, he pities her,
He takes her hands and raises her.
Her head falls upon her shoulder.
When Charles sees she is dead he holds her
Then at once summons four countesses
To take her where she will be best
In the great church of a nunnery
Where all night they watch her and pray.
She is buried beside an altar,
The king can do no more for her.

270   The emperor is back in Aix;
The traitor Ganelon, in chains,
Is there too, in front of the palace;

Serfs have bound up his hands
With leather thongs, he is tied to a stake.
They have beaten him with cudgels and sticks,
The proper reward for such a man.
He awaits his trial as best he can.

271   Charles has summoned his vassals to Aix
From several lands, old records say;
They are assembled at the chapel.
It is a day of festival,
Some say, the feast of St Sylvester.
Then begins the trial and history
Of Ganelon who did the treason.
The emperor first has him dragged in.

272   'Barons,' says Charlemagne the king,
'Here is Ganelon, you must judge him!
He was with me in the army in Spain
And robbed me of twenty thousand Frenchmen,
My nephew Roland, for ever lost,
Oliver, the brave and courteous;
And betrayed the twelve peers for gold.'
Ganelon says: 'It is as you told it.
Roland injured me in my estate,
Therefore I sought his death by right;
But there was no treason in that.'
The French say: 'Perhaps, and perhaps not.'

273   Before the king stands Ganelon,
A noble figure, of fine complexion,
A baron indeed, if he were loyal.
He looks at the French judges, at all
Of them, at the thirty of his kin
Who are with him, and in a clear voice begins:
'For God's sake, barons, hear my case.
I was with the emperor, and in my place
I served him well and loyally.

Roland his nephew hated me
And condemned me to a painful death.
I was to be the messenger
To Marsilie, and when I went there
I used my wits to save myself.
I challenged Roland without seeking help,
And Oliver and all their companions.
Charles heard me, and all the barons.
I took my revenge, but that is not
Treason.' The Franks consider that.

274   Ganelon sees that the judgement begins,
He has with him thirty of his kin.
One, who speaks for the others as well,
Is the lord of Sorence, called Pinabel.
He understands how to put a case
And how to defend his person and place.
Ganelon says to him: 'My friend,
Save me from calumny and a bad end
For I am truly in need this day.'
Pinabel answers: 'Hear what I say:
If any Frenchman says you should hang,
I challenge him with my sword in my hand,
Let the emperor only bring us together.'
Ganelon bows to his rescuer.

275   They take counsel, Bavarians, Saxons,
Poitevins and French and Normans,
Teutons and men from Germany;
The Auvergnois show most courtesy,
They would rather please Pinabel than not.
They say: 'Better let the matter drop.
Let us stop the trial and ask the king
To discharge Ganelon, providing
He serves him in future faithfully.
Roland is dead, and whatever we say
No gold or silver will bring him back.

It would be madness to seek combat.'
The only one who disagrees
Is Geoffrey's brother, by name Thierry.

276 The barons go back to Charlemagne.
They say to the king: 'Sire, we pray
That you discharge Ganelon
So he will again be your liegeman.
Let him live, he is well-born.
Roland will never sound his horn
Again, whatever our verdict may be.'
The king says: 'This is treachery.'

277 When Charles sees all have failed him, he
Bows his head dolorously,
Bewailing his unhappy state.
Then comes Thierry, brother of the great
Geoffrey, a duke of Anjou.
He is lean and light, and wiry too;
Not over-tall and yet not short.
Courteously he speaks in this sort:
'Sire, great king, do not be grieved.
You know how well I have always served;
I owe it to my ancestors
To speak up for the emperor,
And so I do: If Roland had wronged
Ganelon, yet he belonged
To the army and was in your service.
The duty to you should have come first.
Ganelon thought not; he betrayed him;
In doing so he betrayed the king.
Therefore I say he should be hung
And treated like any other felon.
If one of his kin will say I lie
And seeks to prove it, let him try;
My sword will show I speak the truth.'
The Franks find this proposal good.

278 Pinabel has come before the king.
He is tall, strong, brave and quick-moving;
When he strikes he kills his man.
He says to the king: 'Sire, command
Silence. This is your affair.
I see Thierry standing there.
He has lied. I challenge him.'
He hands his right glove to the king
Who says: 'I want hostages.'
Thirty kinsmen pledge themselves.
The king says: 'I will pledge Thierry.'
The kinsmen are put in custody.

279 Thierry sees the battle is on.
He gives Charles the glove from his right hand.
The emperor stands hostage for him
And has four benches brought. There sit
Those who do battle this day.
The challenges are in order. So say
The others, Ogier approves the form.
The combatants ask for horses and arms.

280 When they are ready, they are confessed,
The combatants, and absolved and blessed;
They hear mass and communicate.
They leave the churches land and plate.
Then they go back to Charles. They don
Their strong white hauberks, put their spurs on,
They close their helmets on their heads,
Buckle on swords with golden hilts,
Hang round their necks their quartered shields
And take in their right hands their sharp spears,
Then they mount their swift chargers,
A hundred thousand knights weep. They are
Full of grief for Roland and Thierry.
God knows what the issue will be.

281   There is a great field below Aix.
There the two barons come face to face.
They are both men of great courage,
Their horses are spirited and fast.
They use their spurs and slacken their reins
And attack each other with might and main.
Their shields crack and are shattered to bits,
Their hauberks torn, the girths strain and are ripped,
The saddles turn and fall to the ground.
There are tears from those who stand around.

282   Both knights are down, but neatly
Both of them scramble to their feet,
Pinabel is strong and quick and light.
Neither now has his horse. They fight
Using the swords with golden hilts,
Clashing and striking round their helmets
With blows that are strong enough to make
The helmets echo and the steel break.
The French knights are in mortal fear.
'God,' says Charles, 'Let the right appear!'

283   Pinabel says: 'Thierry, surrender!
And I will be your man for ever
And give you all my worldly goods.
Only, as you can if you would,
Make Ganelon's peace with the king.'
Thierry answers: 'No use talking!
That would be disgrace for me. The fight
Will decide. May God defend the right!'

284   Thierry continues: 'Pinabel,
You are courageous, you fight well
And all your company know this.
Leave this battle where it is,
I'll make your peace with Charlemagne:
But Ganelon must suffer such pain

132

That people will talk of it for ever.'
Pinabel answers: 'By God, never!
I must at all costs defend my kin;
I will not surrender for any man;
Better to die than be disgraced.'
They take to their swords and face to face
Give such great blows that high
Above their helmets the sparks fly.
They cannot be separated now
Until one of them is laid low.

285   He is a hardy fighter, Pinabel.
He strikes Thierry upon his Provencal
Helmet, so that the sparks flash
Enough to set fire to the grass.
He points his sword at Thierry's forehead,
Then suddenly the right cheek is blooded
And the back of the hauberk down to the waist.
God must save Thierry, or he is lost.

286   Thierry feels the wound on his face
And sees blood flowing on the grass.
He strikes a blow at Pinabel's helmet
And carves it to the nose-piece, the head
Is split open, the brains roll out;
Pinabel falls to the ground.
That blow has brought victory.
'A miracle!' all the French cry.
'It is right Ganelon should be hung
And his kin, who pleaded for him.'

287   Thierry has won his battle, the king
Thereupon approaches him
Accompanied by four barons,
Naimès the Duke, Ogier of Denmark,
Geoffrey of Anjou and William of Blaye.
The king folds Thierry in an embrace

And wipes his face with his marten skin
Then throws it off. At once his men
Put another round his shoulders.
Very gently, by the king's orders,
Thierry is disarmed and mounted
On an Arabian mule. Dukes, counts
And all the barons return to Aix
Joyfully. Then begin the forfeits.

288   Charles calls all his counts and dukes:
'What do you think that I should do
With those I took into custody?
They came to support Ganelon's plea
And were hostages for Pinabel.'
The Franks say: 'They should die as well.'
The king says to his officer: 'Go,
And string them all up on the gallows!
By my white beard, if one escapes
You're a dead man.' The officer takes
A hundred sergeants and drags them away;
Thirty of them are hung that day.
Traitors come to a bad end,
Not themselves only, but their friends.

289   Then the Bavarians and the Germans,
Poitevins, Bretons and Normans,
The French above all, are agreed
Ganelon should die in agony.
Four chargers are brought out and
Tied to Ganelon's feet and hands.
The horses are spirited and fast.
Four sergeants drive them past
The spectators towards a stream
That runs through the middle of the field.
Ganelon is lost, his ligaments will
Be stretched intolerably until
All his limbs are torn apart

And his blood flows on the green grass.
He is a traitor; it is not fit
That he should live to boast of it.

290   The emperor has done justice, his rage
Against Ganelon is assuaged.
He has made Bramimond a Christian.
The day has passed, night has come on.
The king lies in his vaulted room;
God sends St Gabriel to him;
This is the angel's message: 'Charles!
Now summon the imperial armies!
March to the city of Elbira
And help king Vivien in Ninfa,
The pagans have besieged these towns.
The Christians call for help.' He groans.
He has no wish at all to go.
'God!' he says, 'My life is sorrow.'
He weeps, tugging his white beard.

So it is Turoldus heard
This history, and so it ends
For he himself is near his end.